W9-BLG-186

NANCY ROTH

A Closer Walk

ꜱꜱꜱꜱꜱꜱꜱꜱꜱꜱꜱꜱꜱꜱꜱꜱꜱꜱꜱꜱꜱꜱꜱꜱꜱꜱꜱ

Meditating on Hymns for Year A

Church Publishing Incorporated, New York

Library of Congress Cataloging-in-Publication Data

Roth, Nancy, 1936–
    A closer walk : meditating on hymns for year A / by Nancy Roth.
        p.   cm.
    Includes bibliographical references and index.
    ISBN 0-89869-303-9 (pbk.)
    1. Hymns—Devotional use. 2. Church year meditations.
3. Episcopal Church—Hymns—History and criticism. 4. Hymns,
English—United States—History and criticsm.   I. Title.
8V340.R68   1998
264'.23—dc21   98-38608
                                                              CIP

The quote from *In Praise of Chaos* by Sean Caulfield is
copyright © 1981 by Paulist Press. Used by permission.

Church Publishing Incorporated
445 Fifth Avenue
New York NY 10016

5 4 3 2 1

Acknowledgments

My thanks are due to Mary Louise VanDyke, custodian of the Dictionary of American Hymnology at the Oberlin College Library, to the writers of hymnal commentaries from many different denominations who have provided me with valuable resources, and to my husband, who spent many hours carefully reading and critiquing the manuscript of this book.

To Bob

Contents

Introduction

When I was in seminary, I enrolled in a church history class taught by the Rev. J. Robert Wright, who gave us the option of either writing an extended book review or meditating on a hymn daily. Choosing the latter, I found that the hymn meditation time was like an adventure. I entered the world of fellow pilgrims—hymnwriters ancient and modern—and discovered them to be interesting and helpful companions on the way.

While the song of the church has been part of my interior life ever since my initiation into the world of hymns at the age of five, belting out "Stand up, stand up, for Jesus" with my Sunday School classmates, it was my seminary assignment that finally became the catalyst for this book of meditations on texts from *The Hymnal 1982*. Each hymn is theology encapsulated in a poem, ultimately given yet deeper meaning by its music.

It is an exercise in humility to look afresh at the texts of our hymns and to ask what they mean. When I began to write commentaries for an earlier publication, *We Sing of God: a Hymnal for Children*, I realized how important it is to take words seriously. The first hymn I encountered, "Morning has broken," sounds to childhood ears like an account of a tragedy at dawn. We cannot take communication for granted.

When we approach hymn texts imaginatively, we look through a window into the life of other Christian communities over the course of many centuries. We understand something of what God and the church meant to them, what the spiritual issues of their time were, and what they urgently needed from God. Contemporary hymns can, in the same manner, expand our horizon to include the companionship of other Christians across the world.

When we take the time to look through the "window" a hymn provides, it does not remain a one-way glass. Gradually, if we take the time, the hymn begins to speak to us as well. It addresses us from across time and space. It begins to speak to our spirits. Through the hymn, we begin to hear the voice of God, and the hymn, in turn, becomes our prayer.

How to Use This Book

This book of meditations is intended to be used in conjunction with *The Hymnal 1982* or *Poems of Grace: Texts of The Hymnal 1982*. The hymns I have chosen follow the pattern of the Church Year, beginning in Advent and including all Sundays and major Holy Days. For this volume, I have chosen hymns suggested for Year A by Marion J. Hatchett in *A Liturgical Index to The Hymnal 1982*. It is our hope that subsequent volumes will follow.

You can read this book randomly, choosing hymns from the Index. But, should you wish to follow the Church Year sequence, I suggest that you "pray" these hymns shortly before the dates indicated, because you will very possibly sing them in church on Sunday.

Although this book is intended primarily for personal devotion, the arrangement of the hymns according to the pattern of the Church Year makes the book useful for sermon and liturgy preparation, as well as for group study and prayer.

PERSONAL DEVOTION

I have used the word "meditating" in the traditional sense of reflecting upon a subject rather than in the more current sense of emptying the mind. The pattern I would suggest for meditating on these hymn texts is adapted from the teaching of St. Ignatius of Loyola:

1. *Preparing*. It is helpful to prepare both physically and spiritually: by settling down in a comfortable position (but not so comfortable you will fall asleep!), centering yourself by paying attention to your breathing, trying to clear the mind of the cares of the day and to focus on the present, and quietly offering this time of prayer to God.

The second part of preparation is, of course, to read the text over, either silently or aloud, from *The Hymnal 1982* or *Poems of Grace: Texts of The Hymnal 1982*.

2. *Picturing*. The first part of each of the meditations is intended to provide some insight into the writers of the hymns, the Scriptural allusions in the texts, and other background that will help the text come alive. During this

part of the meditation, you are listening in your imagination to the voices who first sang it. When did they live? What did they believe? What were their lives like? You are also listening to the Scripture that so often lies behind these hymn texts, and will wish to have a Bible handy.

3. *Pondering.* Pause before continuing on to this part of the meditation, by sitting in silence for a while and perhaps reading the text over again slowly. In this part of the meditation, you are listening to God speaking to you through the hymn. You are letting the words resonate not merely in your intellect and imagination, but in your heart and will.

What might this hymn mean in terms of your life, your faith, your journey with God? Is there some way in which God might be calling you to respond in a specific way to the messages you hear through this text?

The reflections I have written are intended only to be a catalyst for your own thinking and praying. Do not merely read over what I have written, but give yourself time to plumb the depths of the text on your own.

4. *Gathering.* In conclusion, "gather together" your meditation in any way which you find most helpful. You may wish to write your insights in a journal or in the margins of *Poems of Grace.* You may wish to conclude with your own prayer of gratitude to God for the guidance the hymn provides.

5. *Singing.* Although this book is primarily about the texts of the hymns, this does not mean that we think the music is superfluous. Indeed, what inspired this project is the fact that the music is often so compelling that we neglect

to pay adequate attention to the texts. So finally, you may wish to wed words and music by singing the hymn, thereby (in the words of Augustine of Hippo), "praying twice."

You may cover the entire pattern of meditating on a hymn during one prayer session. Alternatively, you can extend the pattern over several days, taking one day, for example, in preparation (reading the hymn and then letting it simmer on your mental "back burner"), one day for "picturing" with the help of the background material, and another for "pondering."

If you say the Daily Offices, you can insert a hymn meditation into Morning or Evening Prayer as a supplementary reading, or add a meditation to Noonday Prayer or Compline.

PREACHING AND LITURGY

If you are responsible for liturgy or preaching, we hope that this book will be a useful resource.

A hymn text associated with the day's lections can provide a fresh approach to preaching, as well as a pastoral way to introduce an unfamiliar hymn. The written meditations in this book can be used as springboards for your own reflection, or you can take the hymn in an entirely different direction. And do not be afraid to ask the congregation to sing at some point during the sermon: you are likely to find new alertness in the pews ever after.

CHRISTIAN EDUCATION

Hymns are an excellent resource for Christian Education because their texts illustrate periods of church history, approaches to theology, and schools of spirituality, as well as providing a lively commentary on Scripture. Quiet days, retreats and adult education series can focus on hymns, using the meditative pattern: preparing, picturing, pondering, gathering, and singing. With the added resource material found in *We Sing of God: a Hymnal for Children* (Church Publishing, 1989), a similar pattern can be used for inter-generational or children's programs.

CONCLUSION

As an addition to the devotional literature of the church, *A Closer Walk: Meditating on Hymns for Year A* will help both individuals and communities to move towards a new appre-ciation of the treasure trove that is *The Hymnal 1982*. The hymns of almost two millennia can be our companions in prayer, helping us to sing in our own hearts the praises of our God:

"So has the Church, in liturgy and song, in faith and love, through centuries of wrong, borne witness to the truth in every tongue, Alleluia!" (Hymn 420, "When in our music God is glorified").

First Sunday of Advent

Hymn 61 and 62*   **"Sleepers, wake!" A voice astounds us**
Philipp Nicolai (1556–1608)

Philipp Nicolai was a Lutheran pastor in Unna, Westphalia. The text of *Wachet auf* was written during the time of a plague which killed over 1,300 people in his region. There were often as many as thirty daily burials in the churchyard beside the parsonage, so it was no wonder that Nicolai's thoughts turned to the life to come. He began the practice of writing daily meditations "to leave behind me (if God should call me from this world) as the token of my peaceful, joyful, Christian departure, or (if God should spare me in health) to comfort other sufferers whom he should also visit with the pestilence. . . ." This collection of meditations, entitled *Freuden-Spiegel des ewigen Lebens* (*A Joyful Mirror of Eternal Life*) contained the text and tunes of what eventually became known as the "King" and "Queen" of chorales: *Wachet auf* ("Sleepers, wake!") and *Wie schön leuchtet der Morgenstern* ("How bright appears the Morning Star," Hymn 496, 497).

---

*Hymn numbers throughout this book are from *The Hymnal 1982*.

The principal biblical reference in the text of *Wachet auf* is to the parable in Mt. 25:1–13, in which Jesus tells the story of ten bridesmaids waiting for the arrival of the bridegroom. Palestinian custom dictated that the bridegroom fetch his bride, with her attendants, from her parents' home to his own. Five of the bridesmaids were wise and had brought extra oil for their lamps; five were foolish, and had not. When the bridegroom was delayed, they slept, only to be awakened at midnight with a shout that the bridegroom was about to arrive. (The sentinel's voice reminds us of Isa. 52:8: "Listen! Your sentinels lift up their voices, together they sing for joy; for in plain sight they see the return of the Lord to Zion.") By now, the lamps of the foolish maidens had gone out, and they had to leave to buy more oil. It was only the wise maidens, prepared with ample oil for their lamps, who joyfully accompanied the bridegroom into the wedding banquet.

The final stanza of the hymn evokes the world of the writer of the Book of Revelation, drawing on the images in chapter 19:6–9: "Hallelujah! For the Lord our God the Almighty reigns. Let us rejoice and exult and give him the glory, for the marriage of the Lamb has come, and his bride has made herself ready."

The translation of *Wachet auf* in *The Hymnal 1982* is by Carl P. Daw, Jr. The tune, written by Nicolai at the same time as the text, appears in two harmonizations: by Praetorius and by J.S.Bach, who used the chorale in his Cantata 140.

ↄ

Once again, the swiftly turning year brings us to Advent, the beginning of the church's calendar. When I was a child in Sunday School, I was taught that Advent was about "the four last things": death, judgment, heaven, and hell. I imagine that "death, judgment, heaven, and hell" were what Pastor Philipp Nicolai was gazing at, as he looked out into his churchyard pitted with so many newly dug graves. He surely awoke, as he never had before, to his own mortality.

"Sleepers, wake!" Most of us are asleep, when it comes to a sense of our mortality. Rushing through our days, trying to meet our own goals and others' expectations, we have little time to think about the end of life. And when we do have to face it, we are ill prepared.

So the sentinels of Advent remind us "Sleepers, wake!" Be ready! For what? For "death, judgment, heaven, and hell"?

No, this Advent sentinel astounds us by calling us, instead, to a wedding feast! We are invited to bring our lamps to welcome the Bridegroom, to hasten through the dark streets towards the gates of pearl to greet him. We can even hear the eager footsteps in the bass line of Bach's harmonization of the chorale. The Bridegroom is Jesus Christ, the Lamb of God. The feast is attended by saints and angels, accompanied by harps and cymbals. The sight is beyond imagining, the sound beyond wondering. We are swept along with the other guests into the city of God.

Perhaps it is easier to face preparing for the end of our lives if we think of the end as a wedding feast rather than "death, judgment, heaven, and hell." But the sentinel call is equally urgent. Be ready! And prepare enough oil for your lamps.

How do we prepare? With what oil can we sustain our light? The spaciousness of the great chorale may give us a hint. If you were to breathe at the pace of the chorale, with an inhalation or an exhalation for each measure or whole note, it might remind you to stop hurrying through life mindlessly. If you were to let the great arc of the melody open your soul to the mystery of God, it might remind you to make one of your priorities in life your relationship in prayer with the Bridegroom whom you are called to greet.

For it is prayer that sustains our light. Prayer that is, above all, a breathing in of the life at the source of our being: God's life and love. And then breathing it out again: God's life and love, into the world.

Praying in preparation for a wedding feast. A good way to begin the year. A good way to prepare for Christmas. A good way to prepare for eternity.

Second Sunday of Advent

Hymn 65   Prepare the way, O Zion
Franz Mikael Franzen (1772–1847)

This hymn is one of the great Advent hymns of the Church of Sweden. Its text is by Franz Mikael Franzen, born of Swedish parents in 1772 in Uleåborg, Finland. Franzen was highly educated, began his career as an academic librarian at Apo, and was ordained in the Lutheran Church at the age of thirty-one. During the Napoleonic wars, Sweden lost Finland to Russia, and Franzen was among the many Swedes living there who left the country to return to Sweden. There, he accepted a call to a rural parish. It was a great adjustment after his stimulating years at the university, but the quieter life gave his abilities as a poet a chance to blossom, and it was there that he wrote some of his finest hymns. Franzen became involved with Archbishop Johan Olaf Wallin in the preparation of a Swedish hymnal, *Svenska Psalm-Boken*, of

1819, described as "a hymnic masterpiece from the golden age of Swedish hymnody,"[1] and was appointed secretary of the Swedish Academy. He was eventually appointed a bishop in Harnosand, a diocese which extended into Lapland, where he worked tirelessly until his death, and was especially concerned with the problem of alcoholism among the nomads of the North.

This hymn was first published in a trial collection of hymns which Franzen helped to edit and with which he made his breakthrough as a hymn writer. The text is based on Isa.40:3–5:

> A voice cries out:
> "In the wilderness prepare the way of the Lord,
> make straight in the desert a highway for our God.
> Every valley shall be lifted up,
> and every mountain and hill be made low;
> the uneven ground shall become level,
> and the rough places a plain."

It is also indebted to Alexander Pope's *Messiah, A sacred Eclogue In Imitation of Virgil's Pollio*, which also has a lively present-tense form.

The hymn came to the United States through the 1958 *Lutheran Service Book and Hymnal*. The melody, which first appeared in the late seventeenth century, probably originates from a sixteenth-century German folk tune.

❧

"Prepare" can be a stressful word during the season before Christmas. But we can't get away from the message, either in the church or in the world outside. We hear the rough voice of John the Baptist preaching in the Judean wilderness,

"Prepare the way of the Lord!" But we also hear the sweet siren songs reminding us there are "only fifteen more shopping days until Christmas." And we hear the laments arising from our own unspoken expectations: "I've always made all the Christmas cookies and the house needs to look perfect."

Preparing for The Perfect Christmas according to the guidelines of a consumer culture or our own lofty ideals is likely to prepare us only for a holiday full of exhaustion, disappointment, and frustration.

There is a different way to prepare. It is to prepare, not just for the holiday called "Christmas," but for the coming of Christ's kingdom in the world. The hymnwriter Franzen reminds us how to do that: we prepare by helping "God's rule" come to earth. The signs of that kingdom are peace, freedom, justice, truth, and love, not only at home but throughout all lands.

Ironically, many of our frantic secular preparations actually militate against that reign. When fatigue makes our tempers fray, love and peace do not abound at home, in the office, or in the marketplace. When we in the affluent Western world spend millions of dollars on luxuries in the name of a Child born in poverty, we are hoarding resources that, in God's kingdom, should be shared more equably with our poorer brothers and sisters throughout the world.

Many Christians are beginning to look at alternative ways of preparing for Christmas. They are making homemade gifts, contributing to a charity in a friend's name, or giving imaginative gifts of service like an evening of baby-sitting, an afternoon of yard work, or a home-cooked meal. They are praying for each of their friends as they address their Christmas cards. They are giving thanks to God for the memories of their lives as they hang the ornaments collected over the years on the Christmas tree. They are trying to reach out to those who are most neglected during this season, through helping in a soup kitchen or joining in a drive to gather gifts for those who would otherwise not receive any.[2]

Most of all, they are preparing by taking time to meditate on the tidings of salvation, perhaps focusing on a phrase like the refrain that concludes our hymn: "Oh, blest is Christ that came in God's most holy name."

This time with God reminds us of the meaning of all the other preparations, providing us with a joy that lasts well beyond the events of this year's holiday, into eternal life.

Third Sunday of Advent

Hymn 75   There's a voice in the wilderness crying
James L. Milligan (1876–1961)

A versatile and prolific writer, James Lewis Milligan was born in Liverpool, England in 1876 and began work in the building trades at the age of twelve, but soon discovered his call to a career in journalism, writing for two London papers and winning a prize for lyric poetry from the University of Liverpool. After he emigrated to Canada in 1911, he continued his career in journalism and became a lay pastor on the Methodist circuit. He was appointed head of the department of public relations for the negotiations that led in 1928 to the union of the Methodist, Presbyterian, and Congregational Churches in Canada and had a great deal to do with the movement's success.

"There's a voice in the wilderness crying," based on Isa.

40:3–11, was written to celebrate that union. One writer has called the hymn "a trumpet call to the new church."[3] We are fortunate to have this hymn, for it is believed to be his only hymn text. The poet's continued success as a journalist made poetry writing difficult; in 1937, it was reported by a friend, "Mr. Milligan says he now has no time for writing poetry, but, 'like Samson, is tied to the grist mill.'"[4]

Dr. Hugh Bancroft, editor of the *Hymnal of the Anglican Church of Canada*, tells the story of a 1938 committee meeting in his home to consider a melody to accompany Milligan's text: "Each one they tried was poor indeed. I suggested that I should go down to the basement, where there was a piano and see if I could evolve something better. I came up about a half hour later with a rough sketch of the tune, *Ascension*."[5]

ও

There is an ancient processional pattern called the "Tripudium": three steps forward, then one step backwards, three steps forward, one step backwards, repeated over and over. I have always thought that the Tripudium mirrors the pattern of life: the times we feel we are moving forwards, and the times when it feels as if we are moving backwards. Most of us prefer advancing all the time, and resent the times our progress is impeded by adversity. But there is a gracefulness in the Tripudium processional which reminds me of the grace-filled moments of our own personal pilgrimages. It reminds me that the backwards step is all right, that it is not a failure, but an opportunity for rest and for gathering momentum for the next step forward.

It is fascinating to walk the Tripudium to the rhythmic meter of "There's a voice in the wilderness crying" and to our last hymn, "Prepare the way, O Zion." The Tripudium is a useful pattern to remember during these days when we are marching towards the end of yet another calendar year, for during this season we often think about the events of our walk through life. The familiar words of Isaiah—"In the wilderness prepare the way of the Lord, make straight in the desert a highway for our God. Every valley shall be lifted up, and every mountain and hill be made low; the uneven ground shall become level and the rough places a plain"—can also be applied to our own stories. When our steps take us through what seems like a rough desert place, or we find an arduous climb looming ahead of us, or we are brought to a complete halt by an obstacle, we may feel like giving up. What is most frightening to us is that we do not know what is ahead: the way is, in the words of Milligan's poem, "untrod."

I imagine that James L. Milligan may have felt the path ahead was impenetrable when he had to go to work at the age of twelve, when a mind like his should have been stretched and nurtured at a fine school. And we can assume that there were many detours and reversals on the road to the Canadian church union for which he worked so assiduously.

What kept him going was what keeps us going, during Advent and throughout our lives, the knowledge that God is with us in our procession. The voice in the wilderness calls out, "Say to those who are of a fearful heart, 'Be strong, fear not! Behold, your God will come. . . .'" The One who comes is strong, yet compassionate, caring for us as a shepherd cares for his sheep. It is that message that keeps us walking—three steps into the future, one step back, three steps forward again, toward the destiny prepared for us by our shepherd God.

Fourth Sunday of Advent

Hymn 56   O come, O come, Emmanuel
Latin, ca. 9th cent.

If you were to attend Vespers at a monastery or convent between December 16 and 23, it is quite likely that you would hear one of the "Great 'O' Antiphons" upon which this hymn is based, sung as an a short verse before and after the Magnificat. Each of these ancient antiphons has a two-fold structure: a salutation using one of the many titles given to the Messiah throughout history, and a petition based on the salutation. Below are English translations of the Latin antiphons, which date from no later than the eighth century, along with their suggested sources in Scripture:

O Sapientia: O Wisdom, you came out of the mouth of the Most High, and reach from one end to the other, mightily and sweetly ordering all things: come and teach us the way of prudence.[6]

Sir.24:3* ("I came forth from the mouth of the Most High, and covered the earth like a mist"); Wis. 8:1 ("She reaches mightily from one end of the earth to the other, and she orders all things well").

O Adonai: O Adonai, and leader of the house of Israel, you appeared in the bush to Moses in a flame of fire, and gave him the law on Sinai: come and redeem us with an outstretched arm.

---

*Ecclesiasticus, or The Wisdom of Jesus Son of Sirach.

Ex.3:2–6 (Moses and the burning bush); Ex.6:6 (". . . I will redeem you with an outstretched arm and with mighty acts of judgment"); Ex.19ff. (the giving of the law on Mount Sinai).

O radix Jesse: O Root of Jesse, you stand for an ensign of the people; before you kings will shut their mouths and for you the Gentiles will seek: come and deliver us, and do not tarry.

Isa.11:10 ("On that day the root of Jesse shall stand as a signal to the peoples; the nations shall inquire of him, and his dwelling shall be glorious"); Isa.52:15 ("so shall he startle many nations; kings shall shut their mouths because of him. . . . "); Rom. 15:11 ("and again Isaiah says, 'The root of Jesse shall come, the one who rises to rule the Gentiles; in him the Gentiles shall hope").

O clavis David: O Key of David, and Scepter of the house of Israel; you open and no one can close, and you close and no one can open; come and bring the prisoners out of the prison, those who sit in darkness and the shadow of death.

Isa. 42:7 ("to open the eyes that are blind, to bring out the prisoners from the dungeon, from the prison those who sit in darkness"); Rev.3:7 (" . . . These are the words of the holy one, the true one, who has the key of David, who opens and no one will shut, who shuts and no one opens").

O Oriens: O Dayspring, Brightness of the light everlasting, and Sun of righteousness: come and enlighten those who sit in darkness and the shadow of death.

Jn.8:12 ("I am the light of the world . . . ."); Heb.1:3 ("He is the reflection of God's glory . . . .");

Mal.4:2 ("But for you who revere my name the sun of righteousness shall rise, with healing in its wings"); Lk.1:79 ("to give light to those who sit in darkness and in the shadow of death . . . .").

O Rex gentium: O King of nations, and their desire, the Cornerstone, uniting both in one: come and save mankind, whom you formed of clay.

Eph.2:14 ("For he is our peace; in his flesh he has made both groups into one and has broken down the dividing wall, that is, the hostility between us"); Eph.2:20 (" . . . with Christ Jesus himself as the cornerstone"); Gen.2:7 ("then the Lord God formed man from the dust of the ground, and breathed into his nostrils the breath of life . . . .").

O Emmanuel: O Emmanuel, our King and Lawgiver, the desire of all nations and their salvation: come and save us, O Lord our God.

Isa.7:14 ("Therefore the Lord himself will give you a sign. Look, the young woman is with child and shall bear a son, and shall name him Immanuel"); Isa.33:22 ("For the Lord is our judge, the Lord is our ruler, the Lord is our king; he will save us"); Mt.1:23 ("She will bear a son, and you are to name him Jesus, for he will save his people from their sins").

This hymn text, by the nineteenth-century hymnodist John Mason Neale, is an adaptation of the "Great O's" rather than a translation. There is a stronger emphasis on the petitions which end each antiphon than in the medieval versions, and a refrain has been added. It has long been associated with its fifteenth-century plainsong tune.

❧

This is the week of the shortest day of the year; the sun seems reluctant to rise and eager to set. No wonder that our ancestors feared this season and built bonfires to lure back the blazing source of light, heat, and life. We may smile at their fear. But no amount of scientific sophistication or astronomical information can protect most of us from the recurrent, though often unconscious, seasonal *angst* of mid-December. Whether it is "light deprivation syndrome" caused by our body's need for the sun, or occasional depression caused by our psyche's fear of mortality, our *angst* mirrors the approaching darkness.

How appropriate it is that the antiphons sung by monastics for twelve centuries during these dark December days convey such urgent longing. They can mirror our own longing, too, if we look at them through the lens of personal experience.

A prayerful way to do this is to write your own "O" antiphons. What do *you* really long for? What aspect of God would you call upon to express that longing? You might base your version on the "Great O's." For example:

O Wisdom, come and bring order in a world that seems full of chaos and confusion.

O Lord of might, come and give me moral courage when I feel helpless and incapable of action.

O Root of Jesse, come and give me the gift of trust in the dependability of God.

O Key of David, come and free me from fear, prejudice, and ignorance.

O Dayspring, come and lighten my burden when the world's foolishness and cruelty overshadow my spirit.

O King of nations, come and bring peace and unity among peoples, races, and families.

O Emmanuel, come and show me that you are indeed "Emmanuel"—God with us.

But you might also want to be more inventive. Here are some poetic contributions from participants who composed their own salutations in a workshop I once led on the "Great O's":

O farthest reach of our souls' imagining, come that we may find the courage to evolve, to strive toward the image in which we were created and have not yet accomplished.

O keeper of time, you come from eternity bearing flesh into Being; come and breathe through our bodies the awareness of your presence, now and always.

O Divine Energy, come and fill me so that I can do the work you call me to do, with skill and with joy.

Our Creator has instilled all this longing in us. The longing is like a magnet drawing us to our Source. It was perhaps the cumulative longing of the human race over the centuries that drew that Source to *us* in a new way almost two thousand years ago, to become, in the Feast of the Incarnation which we shall soon celebrate, "Emmanuel"—God with us.

Christmas Day I (Eve)

Hymn 78, 79   O little town of Bethlehem
Phillips Brooks (1835–1893)

While Phillips Brooks was the thirty-one-year-old rector of Holy Trinity Church, Philadelphia, he planned a trip to the Holy Land. On Christmas Eve, he rode on horseback from Jerusalem to Bethlehem. He wrote in his diary, "Before dark we rode out of town to the field where they say the shepherds saw the star. It is a fenced piece of ground with a cave in it. . . . Somewhere in those fields we rode through, the shepherds must have been. As we passed, the shepherds were still 'keeping watch over their flocks,' or leading them home to fold." Later he attended the Christmas service, which lasted from 10 P.M. to 3 A.M., in Constantine's ancient basilica built over the traditional site of the Nativity. Soon afterwards, he wrote to the children of his parish Sunday School:

> I do not mind telling you (though of course I should not like to have you speak of it to any of the older people of the church) that I am much afraid the younger part of my congregation has more than its share of my thought and interest. . . . I remember especially on Christmas Eve, when I was standing in the old church in Bethlehem, close to the spot where Jesus was born, when the whole church was ringing hour after hour with the splendid hymns of praise to God, how again and again it seemed as if I could hear voices that I knew well telling each other of the 'Wonderful Night' of the Saviour's birth.[7]

The experience made an unforgettable impression upon him; when Brooks returned to the United States, he still had "Palestine singing in his soul." The images of the memorable Christmas Eve in Bethlehem are embedded in a hymn written for a Sunday School Christmas celebration three years later, after he had become rector of Trinity Church, Boston. In America, it is usually sung to the tune ST. LOUIS, composed by Phillips' organist, Lewis H. Redner; in England, it is commonly sung to the folk melody, FOREST GREEN, harmonized by Ralph Vaughan Williams.

Phillips Brooks, one of the most prominent preachers of his time, eventually became Bishop of Massachusetts. But he is remembered today above all for this children's hymn. Its continued appeal to adults as well is proven by its performance at the laying of the cornerstone for Washington Cathedral, in what is now the Bethlehem Chapel.

℘

I was given a Christmas carol book when I was in elementary school. On its cover were children, dressed in wooden shoes and bright old-fashioned costumes, carrying holly and hymn books; they stood in front of a snow-covered Christmas tree and looked extremely happy. When I opened that cover, carol number one was "O little town of Bethlehem." The illustration opposite the music was an expanse of blue and gold, the color of a magical Christmas midnight. Against a cerulean star-speckled sky hovered three blue-robed gold-winged angels. They seemed suspended above the dark streets and shadowy blue buildings—slashed randomly with flecks of yellow to indicate windows—of the town. The picture illustrating "O little town of Bethlehem," written for children about my age (who usually had to be in bed at about the time the mysterious blue shadows of night descended) made a lasting impression.

On the facing page was a carol whose simple and evocative language has remained with me to this day when I think of Christmas. The words which best expressed the amazing angels hovering in the midnight sky were, I thought, "still," "silent," "shineth," and "wondering love." But one phrase struck me above all the others: "be born in us today."

I remember that phrase now when I am bombarded by the sentimentality and commercialism which sometimes accompany Christmas. Despite the noisy throngs in the stores, despite the Santa Clauses and Rudolphs and Little Drummer Boys, despite the pop carols blasting over loudspeakers, the real Christmas "happening" is an event which takes place in the silence appropriate to a birth, the silence of our own souls.

That silence is not lack of sound—a birthing room is full of many sounds, from the encouraging murmurs of husband, nurse, doctor, or midwife to the pushing and breathing of the mother. But the clamor of the outside world has stopped, even time has stopped, and there is only one focus, this work of bringing a child into the world.

The text of the carol, based on a theme reiterated throughout Christian history, turns the birth image topsy-turvy. For the birth of Jesus within us is like a reverse journey of the human birth experience: *we*, our own bodies and spirits, are the "little world" into which God's incarnation comes. We become Bethlehem.

It is to the Bethlehems of ourselves that God presents the wondrous gift of Christ within us. That Christ is not merely the baby Jesus who is depicted, with varying degrees of artistry and truth, in thousands of Christmas cards and carol books. Nor is he merely the earthly Jesus, the great teacher and healer and prophet. He is the Jesus who is everlasting Light, the banisher of our fears, the forgiver of our sin, the enabler of our hope.

Christmas Day II (Dawn)

Hymn 104   A stable lamp is lighted
Richard Wilbur (b. 1921)

It is obvious that this text is the product of a poetic imagination. Its author, educator and writer Richard Wilbur, taught English at Harvard University, Wellesley College, Wesleyan University, and was writer-in-residence at Smith College. As a translator of classical French literature (specifically Molière and Racine) and editor of collections of Shakespeare and Edgar Allan Poe, as well as writer of many books and collections of original poetry, he has received numerous awards and honors, among them his appointment as a United States poet laureate from April 1987 to May 1988. It is no wonder that an elegant and musical sweep of phrase and effortless use of metaphor seem to come so naturally in "A stable lamp is lighted."

The text first appeared in the program for a candlelight service held in the Memorial Chapel of Wesleyan University in Middletown, Connecticut, in December of 1958. The Wilbur family used the poem for their Christmas card that year, and it was subsequently printed in Wilbur's poetry collections of 1968 and 1988.

The hymn is based on Lk. 19:37–40:

As he was now approaching the path down from the Mount of Olives, the whole multitude of the disciples began to praise God joyfully with a loud voice for all the deeds of power that they had seen, saying, "Blessed is the king who comes in the name of the Lord! Peace in heaven, and glory in the highest heaven!" Some of the Pharisees in the crowd said to him, "Teacher, order your disciples to stop." He answered, "I tell you, if these were silent, the stones would [cry] out."

The hymn is set to music written by David Hurd, Professor of Music and Organist at the General Theological Seminary in New York. It is a lullaby reminiscent of nineteenth-century German *lieder* or art-song, underscoring the poignancy of the text.

&

Stones are full of life. The window sills of my study hold a collection of stones, rocks ranging from an iridescent sliver of mica to a large blue-grey stone looking like petrified wood which I picked up years ago above the tree line in Switzerland and hauled all over Europe in my suitcase. My stones hold stories; they are alive with meaning.

They tell the tales of what formed them: lava from a violent eruption, or sandstone compressed with a force that fossilized small sea organisms, or a perfect oval of granite rubbed smooth by the sea. They tell the tales of what they have seen: the stone given me by a friend dying of AIDS, the stone brought to me from the Sea of Galilee, the limestone fragment that once formed part of the south transept of York Minster, burned black and pink in the fire of 1987.

Stones are full of life. As part of the cosmic creation,

surely geological formations were not excluded when the earth sang forth with voices no human ear could hear, as the glow from a stable in Bethlehem lit up the sky. Surely such a response should not be unexpected when God enters human life through a miracle more wondrous than the alchemy which turns straw into gold. Not only shepherds, wise men, Mary, Joseph and the angels, but surely the stones, also, cried out with joy and wonder.

Many years later, other apparently "heavy, dull and dumb" stones felt the sharp percussion of a donkey's hooves, bearing that Child, now grown. They heard the shouts of the people, "Hosanna in the Highest!" and felt the lighter burden of the palms strewn before the Man. And the stones in the Man's path surely joined in the cry of welcome.

Less than a week later, blood-spattered stones trembled along with the rest of creation: "The earth shook, and the rocks were split." (Mt.27:51) And they added their voices to yet other kind of cry: the weeping in mourning for the Man, killed by cruel men whose hearts had "turned to stone."

And every stone shall cry. What message do they cry out? They cry out the Good News: that, in this history of the Man, two worlds are reconciled: the celestial world of the stars bending their voices toward earth, and the world of the stable, the road to Jerusalem, and the bloodied earth on Golgotha.

As a sign of that reconciliation, a great stone, placed at the entrance of a tomb in a garden and rolled away by the power of God, will join on Easter in yet another cry that can be heard throughout the cosmos: "Alleluia! Alleluia! Alleluia!"

Christmas Day III (Day)

Hymn 100   Joy to the world! the Lord is come
Isaac Watts (1674–1748)

Isaac Watts, the son of a nonconformist church deacon, was raised on the Psalms. The story is told that, when his father was imprisoned for his religious views, his mother carried young Isaac in her arms to the prison gate, where she on the outside and he on the inside sang together metrical versions of the Psalms. Later Isaac was to criticize these translations and accept the challenge to write better ones. Instead of being content with a metric translation of the original Hebrew, he set for himself the task of Christianizing the psalm. In making it reflect contemporary thoughts and feelings, he became the creator of the modern English hymn. During his lifetime, he produced about six hundred hymns, a book of *Logic*, and four major theological works.

"Joy to the world"(designated "The Messiah's coming and Kingdom") is the second part of Watt's paraphrase of the last half of Ps. 98:

> Shout with joy to the LORD, all you lands;
>   lift up your voice, rejoice, and sing.
>
> Sing to the LORD with the harp,
>   with the harp and the voice of song.
>
> With trumpets and the sound of the horn
>   shout with joy before the King, the LORD.
>
> Let the sea make a noise and all that is in it,
>   the lands and those who dwell therein.

Let the rivers clap their hands,
and let the hills ring out with joy before the LORD,
when he comes to judge the earth.

In righteousness shall he judge the world
and the peoples with equity.

(The Book of Common Prayer)

This Psalm, a Hebrew song of praise which looks forward to the universal reign of Yahweh, is transformed by Watts into a hymn of joy at the birth of the Messiah.

The music, adapted by Lowell Mason, draws on themes in Handel's "Messiah." The melody for "and heaven and nature sing" can be found in the accompaniment of the tenor aria "Comfort ye my people," and the first four notes of the hymn are identical to the beginning of the chorus, "Lift up your heads, O ye gates." In "Messiah," Handel and his librettist, like Watts, "christened" material from the Hebrew Scriptures so that, ever after, people would identify the texts with the coming of Christ.

❧

In Watts' vision of the redemption of all creation, not only human beings, but the earth itself, rejoices at the birth of the infant King. Heaven and earth sing—literally—in antiphon: fields, floods, rocks, hills, and plains repeat the sounding joy.

This King is greater than the sins and sorrows which choke our lives like an infestation of thistles, remnants of Adam's "curse."

And to the man, [God] said, "Because you have listened to the voice of your wife, and have eaten of the tree about which I commanded you, 'You shall not eat of it,' cursed is the ground because of you; in toil you shall eat of it all the days of your life; thorns and thistles it shall bring forth for you. . . . " (Gen. 3:17–18).

Is the Lord's reign merely a return to an ideal "Garden of Eden"? No: it is a transformation of the present, not a return to the childhood of our race. For this King demands not innocence but righteousness; God's wondrous love calls out for justice.

Just as Isaac Watts transformed a Hebrew Psalm into a Christian poem—just as George Frederick Handel and Lowell Mason transformed a simple descending D major scale into a pattern that sings out "Christmas!"—we have the potential to be transformed by this birth, so that we can contribute to the reign of "truth and grace."

The transformation can begin with learning to listen to "heaven and nature singing." We can open our ears to the sounds of God's creation: to the silence after a snowfall, to the staccato of rain on the roof, to the wind whispering in the pines or whistling down the avenues of our cities. We can hear the sighing of species being exterminated because of our selfish destruction of their habitats, the gasps of the rivers and lakes and seas that are being suffocated with pollutants. We can take time to attune ourselves to our families and friends, to share their times of happiness and grief. We can listen to the voices of the homeless, the abused, and the hungry in our own country, and hear the cries of the victims of war and oppression throughout the world. And we can listen with an appropriate skepticism to the media which attempt to persuade us that we can buy "joy."

The Christmas season at its best can give us many moments of contentment, as we gather with families and friends around firesides, dinner tables, altars, and Christmas trees. But beyond mere contentment lies joy: the joy of discovering that we can be a part of the process of bringing healing to the world beyond ourselves.

The Nativity is merely the beginning of Jesus' path. He will preach the news of peace and justice for all people and enact his message through the terrible and wonderful events of Passiontide and Easter. Are we ready to receive that kind of King?

First Sunday after Christmas

Hymn 82   Of the Father's love begotten
Marcus Aurelius Clemens Prudentius (348–410?); tr. *John Mason Neale* and *Henry Williams Baker*

Prudentius, a Spaniard by birth, practiced law and had a successful career in civil administration, culminating in an appointment to a high position in the court of the Emperor Theodosius. At the age of fifty-seven, he retired to a life of poverty and seclusion in order to devote his remaining years to the writing of religious poetry. This poem, in a translation by John Mason Neale and Henry Williams Baker, is from his *Cathemerinon*, or "hymns of the daily round." This sacred ode celebrates the entire earthly life of Jesus from the Nativity to the Ascension in twelve poems written for use during the hours of day and for special occasions.

Theological discussion in the fourth century was characterized by controversy between two major schools of theology. Theologians of the School of Antioch emphasized the humanity of Christ and the literal interpretation of the

Scriptures, while those in Alexandria emphasized the divinity of Christ and an allegorical interpretation of Scriptures. Prudentius's poetry is a reflection of the questions being discussed in the great church councils, which eventually produced our creeds:

Was Jesus Christ "made" at the time of the Incarnation or was he "eternally begotten of the Father?" *Corde natus ex Parentis, Ante mundi exordium. . . .* ("Of the Father's love begotten, ere the worlds began to be. . . .") Prudentius, using images from Jn.1:1–3 ("In the beginning was the Word"), and Rev.1:8, 21:6, and 22:13 ("I am the Alpha and the Omega"), affirms that Jesus was "eternally begotten of the Father."

Was Jesus really human or did he only appear to be? *O beatus ortus ille, Virgo cum puerpera . . . .* ("O that birth forever blessed, when the virgin full of grace . . . ") Jesus was born of a human woman and was "made man."

How does the Holy Spirit fit in? *Tibi, Christe, sit cum Patre, Hagioque Pneumate . . . .* ("Christ, to thee with God the Father, and, O Holy Ghost, to thee . . . .") The Holy Spirit, the third person of the Trinity, is "worshiped and glorified" with the Father and the Son.

The plainsong, dating from the late Middle Ages, is a Sanctus "trope." Tropes were an embellishment of an older plainsong with more florid extensions of the melody—like a jazz improvisation or a cadenza. The melody line, reaching beyond an octave, mirrors Prudentius' poetic expression of Christianity's credal faith, and helps us reach beyond the words towards the mystery.

When I began seminary, I found the very title of one of the required courses—"Systematic Theology"—to be daunting. On the first day of class, when my pen was poised to begin writing what I expected would be dry abstractions, I was amazed by our professor's opening statement, "This is the most practical course you will take during your years in seminary!"

That statement has proven to be true again and again, especially when I must make decisions or give advice to others about life issues. That is because, as my theology professor was to point out, what we *do* is based on what we *believe*.

Generations of Christians have pondered the mystery of the Incarnation, from those who wrote the Christian Scriptures and argued in the early church councils of Prudentius' day, to those who make the headlines in today's religious controversies. Long ago, I used to be annoyed at these discussions, thinking that belief didn't matter when it came to Christian living. But I was wrong. For example, if I believe that God has chosen only certain elect people for salvation, I will behave differently toward people unlike me than I would if I believed that God cares unconditionally for all human beings. If I believe that God calls us to become purely spiritual, disdaining the things of this world and waiting for bliss in heaven, I will have a different attitude toward a project in environmentally sustainable living than I would if I believed that God loves this earth passionately as part of divine creation.

When Prudentius expressed his faith through poetry, he wrote that "at every hour of the day a believer should be mindful of Christ who is the Alpha and Omega, the Beginning and the End."[8] Pondering the things of God gave meaning to his daily life. For Prudentius, theology was one of the most practical things he could think about, for it opened his soul to the mystery of God and gave meaning to his life.

Pondering theology does not mean that we try to brainwash ourselves into accepting statements that we cannot honestly believe, no matter how cherished they have been throughout the ages. Nor does pondering mean that we need to understand the tenets of our faith with our logical minds. It is helpful to remember that the infinite mystery of the Trinity cannot be limited by any of our attempts to explain it in words. But poetry and music, art and symbol help us direct our attention towards that mystery and to move into relationship with it.

Perhaps we should emulate Prudentius and write our own meditations on the creed, in our own words, whether awkward or poetic, just for ourselves. When these thoughts become our own, we will find that *we* are "doing theology," and that theology is not abstract at all, but, indeed, "the most practical thing we can do."

Second Sunday after Christmas

Hymn 84   Love came down at Christmas
Christina Rossetti (1830–1894)

Christina Georgina Rossetti was the youngest of four children of an Italian refugee from Naples, in exile because of his liberal political views, who was professor of Italian at King's College, London. Christina and her brothers were raised in a heady atmosphere of cultural and political activity. Her oldest brother was the poet and painter Dante Gabriel Rossetti, who was a member of the Pre-Raphaelite Brotherhood. The work of the Pre-Raphaelites, who shared an admiration for Italian painting of the fourteenth century and for Raphael in particular, was characterized by fidelity to nature, moral seriousness, and the frequent use of religious themes or symbolic mystical iconography. Dante Gabriel chose the serious and lovely Christina to pose for the figure of the Virgin Mary in his painting *Ecce Ancilla Domini* (*Behold, the Handmaid of the Lord*), which now hangs in the Tate Gallery in London. Her second brother, William Michael, an author and critic, also was a member of the Pre-Raphaelites. Her sister Maria Francesca, influenced, like their English mother, by the Tractarian Movement—the High Church movement originating at Oxford—eventually entered an Anglican religious community and wrote a scholarly work on Dante.

Ill-health eventually confined Christina to a quiet life, but she was surrounded by the intense activities of the Pre-Raphaelite movement and had already been thoroughly imbued with the spirit of the family. Her poems appeared in magazines and anthologies and were collected by her brother William Michael Rossetti.

"Love came down at Christmas" was first published in *Time flies: a Reading Diary* in 1885. The volume, dedicated to her mother, contains short passages and prose for each day of the year, including this one for "Christmastide." Noted theologian and editor Percy Dearmer describes the text as "this gem, where so much is said in so little space."[9] It is matched to a gentle Irish tune.

ↁ

What are the signs of the coming of Jesus? Christina Rossetti's deceptively simple poem is a play-upon-words which asks that question. We know the answer, of course, when we sing the first word: "Love," which we will sing ten more times in only three short stanzas. For the shepherds and the magi, the angels and the star served as "signs," or signposts, which led them to the manger. We worship that Love Incarnate through the "sacred sign," or symbol, of our love.

Christina Rossetti is surely a member of the spiritual family tree of another retiring English woman many centuries before her, who wrote, "Would you know your Lord's meaning in this? Learn it well. Love was his meaning. Who showed it you? Love. What did he show you? Love. Why did he show you? For love. Hold fast to this, and you shall learn and know more about love. . . . Thus did I know that love was our Lord's meaning."[10] Julian of Norwich, who spent most of her life as an anchoress (or hermit) in a small cell built into the wall of the Church of St. Julian in Norwich, also had abundant time in her solitude to contemplate the signs of love.

When I take the time to contemplate the "signs" of God in this world, I find the same answer suggested by these sisters in the faith. When have I seen the signs of "Love" incarnate? Once I worked one afternoon a week in a high-rise residence for performing artists close to the glittering billboards of Times Square, where flashing signs proclaim the allure of Broadway shows, automobiles, and other symbols of pleasure in our era. When you entered the building, there was another kind of sign. You didn't read this sign with your eyes: you read it with your heart. You read it in the community of people—administration and residents, men and women, young and old, gay and straight, healthy and ill—who had united in a program to support people with AIDS. But this program was more than the sum total of all these people; it was obvious that the residents were, whether they were aware of it or not, doing this difficult work as a channel of a greater Love. When I also became part of that project, I found myself energized and fed by that Love. The more I became a "sign" of that Love in my work there, the more I myself felt, in Julian's words, "wrapped in God's love." In the quiet time on the train going home and walking up the hill to our house from the station, I would find myself enveloped in the thoughts of my afternoon there, warmed by that Love.

There have been other times when, in retrospect, I realized that I had been in the presence of Love incarnate. Sometimes these occasions pass by so quickly that it is difficult to recognize them. Sometimes I just don't take the time to make the connections. The quiet Christina and meditative Julian can teach us all to take the time. When have you seen the signs of Love incarnate? When have you been that sign to others around you? You may find the word "love" occurring more than you expected, when you take the time to ponder that question.

The Epiphany

**Hymn 117, 118   Brightest and best of the stars of the
morning**
Reginald Heber (1783–1826)

Reginald Heber was a child of good fortune and intellect,
born into a home of wealth and culture. At Oxford, he won
two prizes for poetry; he was ordained after graduation and
became rector in the little village of Hodnet in Shropshire,
set in an idyllic pastoral landscape which is reflected in his
poetry. One of his aims was to improve the singing in his
church; he wrote to a friend "My Psalm-singing continues
bad. Can you tell me where I can purchase Cowper's *Olney
Hymns* to put in the seats? Some of them I admire much,
and any novelty is likely to become a favorite and draw more
people to join in the singing."[11] Since he did not find the
hymns he wanted anywhere, he finally resolved to create a
hymnal of his own, intended to be "appropriate to the
Sundays and principal Holydays of the year; connected in
some degree with their particular Collects and Gospels, and
designed to be sung between the Nicene Creed and the
Sermon."[12] The Epiphany hymn "Brightest and best of the
sons of the morning" was first published in the *Christian
Observer*, a periodical edited by Zachary Macauly, Lord
Macauly's father, in November 1811.

Heber spent his last three years as Bishop of Calcutta,
where he died suddenly in a small pool in which he had
sought refreshment after preaching a sermon about the evils
of the caste system. The collection on which Heber had been

working, entitled *Hymns, written and adapted to the Weekly Church Service of the Year*, was published by his widow shortly after his death. It included nine of his own hymns and many contributions by others, among them Milman, Charles Wesley, Arnold, Cowper, Dryden, Addison, Ken and Watts.

When Bishop Heber dedicated a church at Meerut, India, in a "remote situation, in sight of the Himalaya Mountains," he wrote in a letter that he heard this hymn sung better than he had ever heard before.[13] The original manuscript, in Heber's clear, neat handwriting, now in the British Museum, is in a small composition book which may have belonged to one of his daughters, since geometrical problems were found on the backs of the pages.

It is interesting to experiment with the two alternative tunes for this hymn, as Hymn 117 evokes the Victorian England in which the text was composed, and Hymn 118 conjures up the exotic processional of the magi traveling toward the manger.

ᘓ

The human soul needs to worship. Built into our psyche is the desire to pay homage to something beyond ourselves, through giving, serving, or emulating. The word "worship" itself, derived from an Old English word *weorth*, meaning "worth," tells us why. We all "give worth" to something, and act accordingly.

It is quite obvious in childhood. Anyone who has taught pre-school knows only too well, from the children's behavior and dress, what "superhero" is currently in fashion. When I was doing research in children's spirituality, a seminary friend confided to me that as a child she had made little altars in the woods near her home on which she would periodically place M & M's for the magical "little folk" she believed in. Teenagers listen endlessly to their favorite rock stars and try to imitate them in dress and manner, sometimes to the consternation of their parents.

The objects of worship in adulthood may be more difficult to identify. But we can guess what is worshiped, in adults as well as children, by noticing behavior. People who worship money, for example, are likely to expend most of their time and energy in reaching the goal of affluence.

How can we be identified as people who worship Jesus Christ? And how do we find the object of our worship? And then, what do we give him?

We are not the magi, who pled with the "brightest and best of the stars of the morning" to lead them to his cradle. Nor can our costly devotion be expressed solely in the form of incense, myrrh, gold, and jewels.

That infant, grown to manhood, told us how to find him, and how to worship him.

" . . . I was hungry and you gave me food, I was thirsty and you gave me something to drink, I was a stranger and you welcomed me. I was naked and you gave me clothing, I was sick and you took care of me, I was in prison and you visited me. . . . Truly I tell you, just as you did it to one of the least of these who are members of my family, you did it to me." (Mt.25:35–36,40) When we do those things, we act like people who worship the God preached by Jesus Christ.

And we celebrate and renew that identity when we gather to respond to another hint he gave us about how to find him:

"This is my body which is given for you. Do this in remembrance of me."(Lk. 22:19) We find him in giving him our "heart's adoration" in prayer and liturgy, silence and music, and above all in the offering, breaking, and sharing of bread in the Eucharist.

Perhaps the "star of the morning" that led the magi to the cradle in Bethlehem grew and grew, becoming eventually the fire of the Holy Spirit sent at Pentecost by that child, now grown, dead, and risen. When, impelled by our heart's adoration, we follow that star, we will recognize our Lord, act accordingly, and be identified as his.

First Sunday after Epiphany

Hymn 121   Christ, when for us you were baptized
F. Bland Tucker (1895–1984)

In 1982, the General Convention of the Episcopal Church adopted the following resolution:

> The Epistle to the Ephesians admonished the early Christians to "address one another in psalms and hymns and spiritual songs, making melody to the Lord with all your heart." In countless places and through all ages, the Church has continued this ancient tradition of praising God in music. The works of unnumbered poets and musicians, some known but many unknown, have provided the people of God with a goodly heritage of sung praise. Our own branch of the Church in this century has had the uncommon privilege to have among us one of the great hymn writers of this, or any, age: Francis Bland Tucker.[14]

Bland Tucker enthusiastically promoted the work of others, taking an important part in the production of *The Hymnal 1940*. His own hymn texts flowed "like an ever-rolling stream" from his pen during his long and productive life as a priest-poet. His sound classical knowledge, profound theological insights, and sensitive use of language have enhanced English-speaking hymnals around the world.

"Christ, when for us you were baptized" was written when Tucker was seventy-eight years old, in response to a request from an Australian church for a hymn that would reflect the new stress on public baptism. It is based on the story of Jesus' baptism by John in Mt.3:13–17, Mk.1:1–11, Lk.3:21–12, and Jn.1:29–34. In all four of these accounts, the Spirit appears in the form of a dove. Tucker reminds us that the Spirit will also eventually take the form of an "urgent" flame, lighting on the apostles at Pentecost. (Acts 2:3) In the fourth stanza is a reminder of a liturgical action in the Order of Holy Baptism from the Book of Common Prayer—"your cross on us be signed"—and we hear an echo of part of the baptismal covenant—"will you seek and serve Christ in all persons, loving your neighbor as yourself?"

The text is set to a seventeenth–century Scottish psalm tune.

ও

I do not remember my own baptism, which occurred when I was an infant, but I do remember being dressed up in my Sunday best and being taken into New York City for the baptism of my brothers at St. Paul's Chapel of Columbia University, where my father worked. I remember standing with our small family group and hearing the Columbia chaplain, with my youngest brother in his arms, say, "Name this Child." When the godparents replied with his first and middle name,

I can still hear my four-year-old brother's indignant voice supplying our family name, because they had made what was in his eyes the terrible mistake of leaving it out.

How different it is today when I baptize an infant. When we were children, "christening" was a family affair, as my brother had been quick to point out. And now it is a Family affair with a big "F," a celebration in the heart of a parish family, and an initiation into Christ's family, the church.

The baptism of Jesus was no private ceremony; we can safely guess that it took place in the presence of "people from the whole Judean countryside and all the people of Jerusalem" flocking to John the Baptist. (Mk.1:5) Standing in the Jordan with his unkempt cousin, Jesus didn't need solitude in order to hear the voice of God telling him that he was God's beloved, called to do God's work. Jesus listened; he "obeyed his call freely as Son of Man to serve and give [his] life for all."

That is what our baptisms tell us: we are God's beloved and we are called to do God's work. When we are baptized with Jesus' Spirit, we are signed by the cross which describes the paradox of his life: the intersection of suffering and redemption, the Crucifixion and Easter, service and freedom.

Those last words remind me of the ancient Collect for Peace from the Sarum missal which is said at Morning Prayer:

"O God, who art the author of peace and lover of concord, in knowledge of whom standeth our eternal life, whose service is perfect freedom . . . ."

When, after the baptism, a congregation responds, "We receive you into the household of God. Confess the faith of Christ crucified, proclaim his resurrection, and share with us in his eternal priesthood," I know that God's family has grown. When I carry a baby up and down the aisle of a parish church during the "Peace" which follows, and look at the faces of the child's church family, I know that we are all rejoicing in a new life of service and of freedom.

Second Sunday after Epiphany

Hymn 443   From God Christ's deity came forth
Ephrem of Edessa (4th cent.)

Ephrem of Edessa, Syrian teacher, poet, orator, and defender of the faith, was born around 306 in Mesopotamia and was baptized at eighteen by James, Bishop of Nisibus, who may have taken him to the Council of Nicaea in 325. When the Persians captured Nisibus, Ephrem moved to a cave in the hills above the city of Edessa, where he wrote most of his spiritual works. He lived on barley bread, dried herbs, and occasional greens; he drank only water, and his clothing was a mass of patches. However, he was not a recluse; he often preached in Edessa, a center for the spread of the Gospel in the East long before the conversion of the western Roman Empire.

During a famine in 372–373, he distributed food and money to the poor and tended the sick, which may have brought on his death from exhaustion.

Ephrem discovered that hymns could be of great value in the work of evangelism, and used his texts, sung by a choir of women, to oppose those of the Gnostic heretics. His hymns were very popular and gave rise to a new style of Greek sacred music.

He was the voice of Aramaic Christianity, speaking the language that Jesus spoke and using the images Jesus used.

His known writings include eight groups of hymns, as well as a commentary on Genesis and a study of Jesus. Wishing to show the scope of Christian hymnody in varied cultures, the compilers of *The Hymnal 1982* asked Howard Rhys of Sewanee to translate some of Ephrem's hymns, and F. Bland Tucker selected five stanzas from the first hymn in Ephrem's collection for Easter.

The structure of "From God Christ's deity came forth" consists of four poetically balanced lines, each dealing with one attribute of Christ's identity, and concluding with a refrain of praise which sums up the theme of the preceding lines. The music reflects this structure: a statement is followed by sequential phrases building up to the climax, a brief, bold refrain. The hymn is full of scriptural references: ten from the Gospels, three from Paul's writings, one each from the Psalms and from Hebrews.

❧

The Epiphany season is rich with examples of the manifestation—or *epiphaneia*—of Jesus' deity, or divine nature. In these first weeks, we read the stories of the magi's homage and of the voice from heaven above the river Jordan proclaiming "This is my beloved Son." But these obvious examples do not exhaust the concept of *epiphaneia*.

Ephrem of Edessa understood that "epiphany" is woven throughout Jesus' life, from the miracle at the wedding feast through the ascension. The five refrains of his hymn sing the praises of Jesus' "Oneness," "teaching," "mercy," "coming," and "glory." Those attributes were signs of deity, both revealed and veiled in the events of one extraordinary life.

But Epiphany is not just a season when we remember past events, any more than Christmas and Easter are merely commemorations of something that happened long ago. God did not cease manifesting the divine nature in the world after the ascension of Jesus. If we have eyes to see them, *epiphaneia* are woven throughout our hours and our days. And the praises of Ephrem can help us discover them.

For example, because we live in a time of fragmentation and separation, we crave God's gift of "Oneness." Sometimes there is a manifestation of "oneness" in our individual lives, perhaps when our work or our prayer engages us with such attention that we sense what it means to be an integrated human being, with mind, heart, body, and spirit working together as one.

Sometimes we experience that kind of unity in our communities. If we are fortunate, we experience it in the church. I am reminded of the splendid liturgy at the Investiture of Presiding Bishop Frank Griswold, in which Native American drums, African-American spirituals, and the best of Anglican church music created an atmosphere of "oneness" that could never have been achieved through homogeneity.

What moments of *epiphaneia* do you remember in your life?

Perhaps you have been inspired by ideas which reflect Jesus' "teaching." This teaching—perhaps about stewardship of the earth, or the peaceful settlement of international disputes—may not come from "religious" people, but that does not mean they are not the thoughts of God.

Perhaps your epiphanies have been moments when you experienced God's "mercy" and knew you were loved, or when you were finally able to forgive someone. Perhaps they were times when you realized that God's "coming" to earth in human flesh meant that you also, as a human, must be of infinite value in God's eyes. Or maybe you have glimpsed God's "glory" in nature, a beloved friend, or great music.

These experiences transform our perception of the world and of God. But most of all, they transform us. As the collect for this Sunday prays, "Grant that your people . . . may shine with the radiance of Christ's glory." For it is not only Jesus who revealed the divine nature. We ourselves, made in the image of God, are meant to do so as well.

Third Sunday after Epiphany

Hymn 549, 550   Jesus calls us; o'er the tumult
Cecil Frances Alexander (1818–1895)

Cecil Frances Humphreys was born in County Wicklow, Ireland, in 1818; her father was a Royal Marine, landowner and government agent. She published two popular collections of hymns for children before her marriage, during which time she and her sister ran a school for deaf-mutes. The profits from her *Hymns for Little Children* were designated for the school. She was a well-educated churchwoman, keenly interested in the Oxford Movement, who attended daily services and devoted time to the unfortunate. In 1850 she married the Rev. William Alexander, one of the most brilliant men in the Irish church, who became Bishop of Derry and Raphoe and, after his wife's death, primate of all Ireland.

Cecil Frances Alexander was to write 400 hymns, most of them for children. Her children's hymns are characterized by the use of images to capture a child's imagination, followed by instruction couched in simple language expressing theological truths. It has been said that "few women of her time understood the psychology of childhood as well as she."[15]

"Jesus calls us," although not written specifically for children, conveys the same sense of immediacy as her children's hymns. First published in a volume issued by the Society for the Promotion of Christian Knowledge, it was written for St. Andrew's Day shortly after the author's marriage, when she was living in a remote parish in County Tyrone. The Scriptural allusions include Mt.4:18–19, Mk.1:16–17 (the calling of Simon Peter and Andrew), and Jn.21:15 ("When they had finished breakfast, Jesus said to Simon Peter, 'Simon son of John, do you love me more than these?'"). The two tunes provided in *The Hymnal 1982* have very different emotional flavors which express two aspects of Jesus' "call" to us. The first, by David Hurd, has a subjective and pensive tone, while the second, a folk-like melody from *The Southern Harmony*, is objective and energetic.

の

"Jesus calls us." When I look back over my own life, I realize that Jesus' call was not a one-time "summons" to me, any more than it was to the fishermen Andrew and Peter, interrupted in the midst of casting their nets into the sea.

It has been said that a voyage of a thousand miles begins with one step. The two rough fisherman responded by taking that step, right into the water and up onto the beach. But Jesus had to "call" to them over and over during their wandering the dusty roads of Galilee together, teaching them in strange parables, revealing to them his power over physical and mental illness, stilling their fears in the midst of a sudden storm on a lake, asking them to distribute five loaves and two fishes to a crowd of five thousand. Jesus called to them in Gethsemane, on Golgotha, in the Easter garden, on the road to Emmaus, and from the mount of the Ascension.

So it is with most of us. There was a first "call"—or experience of Jesus as a real presence in our life. It is the time when all we have learned about God becomes transformed into a relationship with God. John Wesley described the moment in his famous description of his experience during Moravian worship at Aldersgate: "My heart was strangely warmed." But that sensation of warmth was only the beginning of discipleship for John Wesley, just as the plunge from his boat into the sea was only the beginning of Andrew's path.

I remember in my life those first intuitions which were the "call" to priesthood. I remember following them by going to seminary and becoming ordained. I remember thinking, "Well, that's it. I've followed 'the call.'" But I soon found out that the "calls" continued, that I have to continue to listen to those intuitions in order to discover where God needs me. I have discovered that Jesus never stops calling.

Whatever our calls to ministry, whether we are lay or ordained, we need to continue to listen. The calls we hear may be quiet and subtle, like the David Hurd tune for this hymn; Jesus may call us to pray for someone, to write a letter, or to spend more time in prayer. Or they may be active and obvious, like the tune from *Southern Harmony*: someone may come to your door asking for help, a member of your family may fall ill and need your care, or a political issue may catch your attention.

One thing is sure. Jesus calls us, and will continue to call us, throughout our lives, until he calls us into his presence in eternity.

Fourth Sunday after Epiphany

Hymn 554 'Tis the gift to be simple
Shaker Song, 18th cent.

The United Society of Believers in Christ's Second Coming, a sect originating about 1706 in Manchester, England, was soon labeled the "Shaking Quakers" because of the trembling which marked their worship. In 1774, their leader, Mother Ann Lee, believed by them to be the female incarnation of Christ, led a group of Shakers to America, and soon there were twelve communities in New York and New England. Early in the following century, communities were founded in Kentucky, Ohio, and Indiana.

Shaker communities became one of America's marvels and were visited by many foreign observers. Life in the Shaker villages seemed idyllic, with elegantly simple buildings, graceful furniture, large cattle herds, flourishing gardens and abundant food. Life within the community was peaceable and minutely regulated, with the sexes separated so far as practicality would permit.

By the end of the nineteenth century, however, Shakers had become a mere remnant. Their legacy remains in some of their inventions—such useful items as the flat broom, the washing machine, the clothespin, the apple corer, and the first metal pen points—in the beautiful design of their furniture, and in their music, of which this hymn is the best known example.

Shakers put a high value on the concept of "laboring," whether laboring in the workplace or field for the benefit of the society, or laboring in vigorous dance movements during worship. These were often based on a shuffling step and were used in order to awaken spiritual gifts. Laboring was "joyful exercise . . . mighty through God, joyful as heaven, and solemn as eternity."[16]

Early manuscripts of "'Tis the gift to be simple" identify the song as a "Quick Dance," but there is no composer or author cited. Some evidence points to a certain Elder Joseph Brackett, Jr., who sang it at a number of Shaker societies in the summer of 1846.[17] The modern popularity of the tune is due largely to its use in the seventh section of Aaron Copland's *Appalachian Spring*. In 1996, the Music Educator's National Conference named "Simple Gifts" one of the forty-two songs that every American should know.

∽

The idea that body-language is a part of worship is not as foreign to Episcopalians as we may at first think. Our worship, like that of the Shakers, is anything but sedentary! Rather than shuffling and spinning, we kneel, sit, and stand to express various attitudes of devotion, and we walk to the altar and hold out our hands to receive communion. We are usually not conscious of the great degree in which the position of our body affects our emotions, but if we should have the courage to experiment with kneeling during the sermon, the connection between body and spirit would soon be clear.

Dance historians have paired certain movements with "'Tis the gift to be simple," and I often use them in the workshops I teach about the integration of body and spirit. The movements can become a kind of movement prayer using the text of "'Tis the gift to be simple."

The first half of the hymn consists of four steps forward and four back, a pattern which is then repeated. The arms make "scooping" movements when you walk forward, and when you walk backwards, you shake your arms vigorously.

The Shakers believed that the "scooping" movements gathered blessings, and that the shaking movements got rid of evil. How appropriate that these movements are set to the words that describe the simple freedom of knowing "where we ought to be." When you scoop your arms, mentally picture gathering the blessing of knowing yourself loved by God. When you shake your arms, picture yourself shaking off those things that get in the way of the blessing of God's love. To know the "simple" truth enacted through this scooping and shaking is freedom. When we learn to move through life in the context of that freedom, we know we are in "the place just right."

When we are in that place, we need no longer be rigid with fear and defensiveness. Instead, like a resilient tree in a gale, we can bow and bend—which we do during the next four measures, stepping to each side with arms outstretched to the side, then bowing forward with our hands joined in prayer. These movements teach us that is not shameful to "give in" to others, but that true harmony comes from mutual listening and flexibility.

Moreover, if we truly allow ourselves to be moved by the Spirit, we may find that we are called to change. We may even come full circle in some of our opinions. In the final four measures, as we turn around clockwise and then counterclockwise, with our hands raised at shoulder level like a priest at the altar, we will remind ourselves that "coming round right" doesn't necessarily mean standing our ground. It may, indeed, mean taking many detours.

It is a gift to be able to move in freedom to the rhythm of a hymn text like this one from the Shakers. When we do this "joyful exercise," the wisdom in the text becomes part of our body's experience as well as our soul's.

Fifth Sunday after Epiphany

Hymn 488   **Be thou my vision, O Lord of my heart**
Irish, ca. 700, versified *Mary Elizabeth Byrne (1880–1931)*;
    tr. *Eleanor H. Hull (1860–1935)*

This prayer from the Irish monastic tradition is an example of a Celtic "lorica" or breastplate, an incantation to be recited for protection.

The Celtic church existed in the British Isles long before the mission of St. Augustine from Rome to Canterbury in 596–597. Its origins are lost in the mists of time, but it is likely that the first Christians to visit Britain and Ireland were probably traders from the Mediterranean; even during the lifetime of Jesus, trade was well established between the Middle East and the British Isles.

With the coming of the Saxons in the fifth century, the Celtic church and its culture almost disappeared, and the Christian communities that survived in Cornwall, Wales, Ireland, and Scotland were cut off from intercourse with Rome and the Continent. It was in part because of that isolation that the Celtic Christians found it difficult to accept the Roman version of Christianity that St. Augustine brought. They finally submitted in 664 at the Synod of Whitby to the rule of the Roman Church.

Fortunately, the Synod of Whitby was not the last word for Celtic Christianity. It has captured the imagination of present-day Christians and has made a strong impact on contemporary spirituality. Today's Christians who seek to include environmental justice as part of their ethical practice can claim kinship with the Celts, who understood that this world is God's world and that nature and grace are intertwined.

In our present-day search for a spirituality that sanctifies the ordinary moments of our lives, we are learning much from the Celts, who saw the routine tasks of daily life as permeated with the sacred. Moreover, they understood Christ's cross—like the High Crosses in the Irish countryside—as a cross of victory over evil. That idea gives redemptive meaning to humanity's suffering today throughout the world.

We are attracted by the optimism of the Celts. It has been suggested that the very early conversion of the Celtic peoples meant that they received the gospel at a time when the Church emphasized the goodness of God, who healed and restored the whole of human nature, as well as the whole creation.[18]

The Bible was the Celts' main book of study. It is clear that the author of "Be thou my vision" knew Col.1:15–23 ("He is the image of the invisible God. . . . "); Col.2:2–3 (" . . . Christ himself, in whom are hidden all the treasures of wisdom and knowledge"); and Gal.2:20 (" . . . it is no longer I who live, but it is Christ who lives in me.")

The poem, over a thousand years old, was versified by Mary Elizabeth Byrne, a graduate of the National University of Ireland. She worked from a prose translation by Eleanor H.Hull, the founder and honorary secretary of the Irish Text

Society, who was instrumental in promoting a reawakened interest in early Gaelic culture. It is sung to an Irish folk melody named after a hill—Slane—associated with Patrick, one of Celtic Christianity's great saints.[19]

∾

What does it mean for Christ to "be our vision"?

In our era, human beings relate to the world—more than at any other time in history—through vision. We get most of our information through looking: at computer screens, books, magazines, newspapers, and the network news. Much of our entertainment is watching: television, sports, movies. Even in the course of one day, we are likely to travel farther away from the familiar sights of home than people have ever done before. The world of advertising utilizes the power of our sense of sight by luring us, through subtle visual suggestion, into a state of dissatisfaction with what we have so that we will buy something we think we want.

We are likely to see, "waking or sleeping," these images which swirl around us. Do you ever find that, even in your dreams, the accumulated images of the day parade in an unending procession through your brain?

What if Christ were our "vision," "our best thought, by day or by night"? And how can we learn that kind of vision?

We do that by looking at the world through new lenses. These lenses are not optical glass; they are "spiritual" lenses. They are not a change of prescription; rather, they are a change of perception. When we put them on, we see, in the light of the "bright heaven's Sun," that the material world is shining with God's presence.

We discover that presence, not merely with our eyes, but with all our senses. In the words of a Celtic prayer:

Bless to me, O God,
   Each thing mine eye sees;
Bless to me, O God,
   Each sound mine ear hears;
Bless to me, O God,
   Each odour that goes to my nostrils;
Bless to me, O God,
   Each taste that goes to my lips,
   Each note that goes to my song . . . .[20]

The Celts knew that the sacred presence hovered over their daily chores:

"I will kindle my fire this morning in the presence of the holy angels of heaven . . . "
"Bless O God my little cow, Bless Thou my partnership and the milking of my hands, O God."
"Bless, O Chief of generous chiefs,
   My loom and everything a-near me."[21]

Our perception that the holy is not something separate from ordinary life, but embedded in it, helps us "bless" our own daily activities.

Why not go through your day's activities in your mind, and write your own "blessings"? ("I will make my bed this morning in the presence of the holy angels of heaven"; "Bless my hands at this computer, O God".) It just might improve your vision, and certainly would deepen your love of the "Heart of your heart," through whom you see, and in whom you dwell.

Sixth Sunday after Epiphany

Hymn 641   Lord Jesus, think on me
Synesius of Cyrene (375?–414?)

Synesius was born in Cyrene (now part of Libya) between 365 and 375, to a prominent pagan family who claimed descent from Spartan royalty. As a young man, he studied with the brilliant mathematician and Neoplatonist Hypatia in Alexandria.

Neoplatonism was a philosophical system devised by Plotinus and inspired by Plato. The main purpose of the Neoplatonists was to provide a sound intellectual basis for a religious and moral life. They sought the Absolute who lies behind all reality, the One who, according to Plotinus, "has its centre everywhere but its circumference nowhere." They believed that one could know that Absolute only by the method of abstraction, divesting one's experience of all that is specifically human.

Synesius found the mystical emphasis of Neoplatonism to be compelling and began writing mystical verse. He returned to Cyrene after his studies in Alexandria, but soon was asked to head an embassy from the cities of his region to the imperial court in Constantinople. It was here that he became a convert to Christianity. After returning once again to Cyrene, he married a Christian wife and took up a life of "books and the chase" on a provincial estate.

When he was chosen bishop of the neighboring city of Ptolemais in 410, he at first hesitated to accept, since he wished to continue living with his wife and to retain certain of his Neoplatonic philosophical beliefs (for example, in the pre-existence of the soul and the eternity of the world). Eventually, without committing himself to give up either his wife or his doctrines, he was consecrated by Theophilus, Patriarch of Alexandria.

Most of Synesius' writings date from his pre-Christian period. "Lord Jesus, think on me," however, is based on an epilogue to his first nine Christian odes. C. S. Phillipps considers the odes as "of great interest and beauty in their presentation of Christian devotion as seen through the eyes of a Platonist philosopher."[22]

The somber translation, by Allen William Chatfield, from his *Songs and Hymns of Earliest Greek Christian Poets*, was considered by Chatfield to be "a paraphrase or amplification rather than an exact translation of the original." The tune is unique among early English psalm tune repertory in having plaintive repeated notes, which are very appropriate to the penitential nature of the text. Both tune and text are familiar to the contemporary musical world through their use by Benjamin Britten in his score of the church drama *Noye's fludde*, a setting of the Chester Miracle Play.

೧೨

If you attend Benjamin Britten's *Noye's fludde* for the first time, a surprise is in store for you. For as soon as you settle down in your seat or lean back in your pew, ready to relax and watch and listen, you find that the entire congregation is obliged to stand and sing "Lord Jesus, think on me, and purge away my sin"—the entire hymn, all the way to "that, when the flood is passed, I may the eternal brightness see, and share thy joy at last." Meanwhile, out of the corner of your eye, you glimpse Noye (or Noah) walking through your midst to the empty stage, where he kneels to hear the voice of God: "I see my people in deede and thoughte Are settle full fowle in synne." Thus begins the medieval —yet very contemporary—drama of the consequences of "synne," or sin.

You soon see the story of a flood which engulfs the world and destroys all except those aboard that strange ship, "three hundreth cubettes longe, and fiftie brode, to make yt stronge." Yet Noye and his family are safe in the ark, riding on the destructive waves. You are relieved, because, very early in the drama, the hymn has invited you to become a participant rather than a spectator, and to seek refuge with the unusual passengers in that symbolic vessel.

I am glad we have the story of the flood in our Bibles. It reminds me of the Ark where I can find shelter when I feel in imminent danger of drowning.

I suspect that it was the Ark that was lacking in the philosophy Synesius of Cyrene studied so assiduously in the years before his conversion to Christianity. "Divesting one's experience from all that is specifically human" doesn't always work when our very human capacity for pride, covetousness, lust, envy, gluttony, anger and sloth threatens to swamp our emotional and spiritual equilibrium. "Seeking the Absolute through abstractions" doesn't help us keep afloat in a world in which tidal waves of evil threaten life itself.

No, we need an ark, an ark called Jesus. We need to know that the Absolute "thinks on us," through the proof given us by the Incarnation. We need to know God in human life. We need Good Friday. We need Easter. We need to know that when we confess our harmful passions and corroding sins, we can indeed be forgiven and healed. We need to know that there is Rest at the end of our travail, that there is a Goal at the end of our wanderings.

Above all, we need to know that our turbulent worlds, both the one in our hearts and the one outside us, are not the only worlds there are. We need to know that there is awaiting us, at the end of our time on earth, an Ark illumined by eternal brightness, whose building specifications we cannot even imagine. We do know that it will have something to do with the Lord Jesus who "thinks on us" both during our lives and afterwards. We also know that we will continue to share the joy of the voyage which began when we first turned towards him.

Seventh Sunday after Epiphany

Hymn 516   Come down, O Love divine
Bianco da Siena (d.1434?); tr. *R. F. Littledale (1833–1890)*

Bianco da Siena, born in the middle of the fourteenth century, was trained as a worker in wool. His profession may have earned him his nickname, meaning "white." In 1397 he joined a group first known as *poverelli di Cristo* and later as *Compagnia dei Gesuati*, and lived in their community in Venice. Members of the group were laity who followed the Augustinian Rule and had a great interest in mysticism. The latter caused them to be distrusted by authorities at the Vatican, who feared they might drift into heresy.

Bianco was an ardent poet, who wrote with the intention of strengthening the faith of his brethren. His texts were examples of *laudi*—the extremely popular Italian vernacular hymns of praise and devotion, dating from the time of Francis of Assisi. Congregations called *Companie de Laudesi* or *Laudisti* formed to cultivate this type of devotional singing among the Italian people. It was out of the musical and dramatic representations occurring in their meetings that the oratorio was to develop in the sixteenth century.

In 1851, these hymns were gathered into a collection entitled *Laudi Spirituali*, where they were discovered by English priest and writer R. F. Littledale, a friend of the Pre-Raphaelites, who saw the Middle Ages as a halcyon era for Christianity. Littledale translated this exquisite text for a collection entitled *The People's Hymnal*:

> *Discendi, amor sante*
> *Visita la mie mente*
> *Del tuo amore ardente,*
> *Si che di te m'infiammi tuto quanto.*
>
> *Vienne, consolatore,*
> *Nel mio cuor veramente:*
> *Del tuo ardente amore*
> *Ardel veracemente. . . .*

Seeing these words out of context, one might expect them to be part of the libretto for a love aria from a dramatic opera. Instead, they are a hymn text, appropriately paired with music by Ralph Vaughan Williams which conveys the soul's breathless desire for God in the urgent rush of the quarter notes that end the second and fourth phrases of each stanza.

❧

Love poetry and the poetry of mysticism can be almost indistinguishable one from the other. Over the centuries, Christian mystics have used erotic images to express their desire for union with the divine. Among these images, the symbol of fire was called upon often to express the threefold mystic journey of purgation (being cleansed of sin), illumination (growing in knowledge and love of God), and union (being united spiritually with God).

To understand the power of that image, we need to imagine the world before the invention of electric lights, when most light, with the exception of the moon, was produced by fire, and all light was hot.

The fire that illuminated darkness and provided warmth also had the capacity to destroy. Its power to purge the impurities in metal is used by Bianco to illustrate his desire to be "consumed" by his ardor for God: *Arda si fortemente Che tuto mi consumi*. (Littledale translated these lines into the more properly Anglican "till earthly passions turn to dust and ashes in its heat consuming.") Bianco prayed to have all that was *not* of God in him burned away; it was the way he sought his true humanity. It has been said that "anyone who has seen gold being refined knows how beautifully the fire flames up through the gold as it burns the dross and melts the gold. As the gold liquefies, it seems to blossom like a marvelous golden flower."[23]

This is strong language, but does it not express our own most basic longing, when we are quiet enough to think about it, the longing to be united with our Source?

The path of our ordinary lives as Christians is not so far removed from the mystic's path. It begins when love awakens within us, when God becomes to us as real as those more obvious everyday realities which surround us. It continues as love helps us turn from the bondage of selfishness, pride, and greed. Our love makes us take ever greater delight in realizing that God shines through every moment of our daily lives. Along with the illumination that this knowledge gives us, is another illumination: the glow of our hearts, as we give ourselves in service to others.

The mystic way is not reserved for the extraordinary saints of God or for the poets, like Bianco, whose work has survived. The great teacher of prayer, Evelyn Underhill, describes mysticism as "the art of union with Reality."[24] Isn't that what we all want? We find our truest selves when we ardently seek God and become attuned to God's love, so that its fire permeates our life.

Eighth Sunday after Epiphany

Hymn 695, 696   By gracious powers so wonderfully sheltered

F. Pratt Green (b.1903); after Dietrich Bonhoeffer (1906–1945)

Dietrich Bonhoeffer was the son of a noted Berlin physician and grew up in a secure, literate, and cultivated family atmosphere. He was educated in Tubingen and the University of Berlin, and in 1930 spent a year at New York's Union Theological Seminary, where Reinhold Niebuhr recognized him as "a brilliant and theologically sophisticated young man."[25]

Dismayed by Hitler's persecution of the Jews, he returned to Germany and became a leader of the Confessing Church, a group of Protestants openly opposed to the German Lutheran Church, which had reached an "understanding" with the Hitler's National Socialists. In February

1933, he denounced on the wireless the corrupt political system which made the *Führer* its idol. He spent the years between 1933 and 1935 in London, where he ministered to two German congregations and tried to explain to his British friends, among them Bishop Bell of Chichester, the true character of the struggle in Germany.

Returning to Germany, Bonhoeffer taught at an underground seminary for pastors of the Confessing Church at Finkenwalde, where he said to his students, "Only those who cry out for the Jews may also sing Gregorian chant."[26] In June 1939, American friends got him out of Germany, but soon he felt he had to return to the struggle in his own country. Bonhoeffer never regretted this decision, even in prison, where he was to write, "I am sure of God's hand and guidance . . . .You must never doubt that I am thankful and glad to go the way which I am being led."[27]

As a result of his involvement in an unsuccessful plot to assassinate Hitler, Bonhoeffer, his sister Christine, and her husband, Hans von Dohnanyi (father of conductor Christoph von Dohnanyi), were arrested by the Gestapo on April 5, 1943. In prison, the guards so respected him that they secretly helped him visit other prisoners to comfort them, safeguarded his papers, and helped him communicate with his family.

The text of Hymn 695, which was given shape as a hymn by British hymnwriter F. Pratt Green, was found in a letter dated December 28, 1944, addressed to Bonhoeffer's mother, who was to celebrate her seventieth birthday two days later. It is one of the most moving expressions of faith to come out of the horrors of World War II.

On Sunday, April 8, 1945, a few minutes after conducting worship for his fellow prisoners, he was taken away by two civilians. His final words to his friends were, "This is the end, but for me it is the beginning of life." He was hanged the next day.

ↄ

When you enter Salisbury Cathedral, your eye is drawn to a magnificent stained glass window at the east end, a sea of blue glimpsed through a forest of grey columns. It is a modern window, made in Chartres. Walking towards it down the long grey nave and around the ambulatory, one begins to discover the design. It is the "Prisoners of Conscience Window," celebrating the martyrs of our faith across the centuries.

The experience of standing before that window is humbling. I have always been in awe of martyrs. I have never been a risk taker. I do not like standing at the edges of cliffs or driving on icy roads. I have always had a keen sense of my own mortality and I love to be alive. The desire for martyrdom is not part of my psychological profile. So I feel very insignificant when I come face-to-face with the Christian martyrs. How could they be so brave?

I think about what circumstances might cause me to give up my own life, and it occurs to me that my children's survival would be something I would die for. I love them with all the energy of my being, and there is no way that I could be persuaded to betray them on account of my own survival. Yes, I might be willing to be stoned, like the first martyr Stephen, or to go to the gallows, like Dietrich Bonhoeffer, for them.

I think the martyrs must have felt the passion for God that a mother feels for her children.

How did they have the courage, I wonder? And how did Dietrich Bonhoeffer have the courage to write that he was "by gracious powers so wonderfully surrounded," when most people in his situation would have been in despair?

Then I remember the derivation of the word courage. Right in the heart of the word is the French word *coeur*, the heart. The martyrs could be brave because their hearts were like the heart of a mother on fire for her offspring.

The martyrs' hearts blazed with the fire of their love for the God who sustained them, through imprisonment, torture, and death. Dietrich Bonhoeffer was able to be pastor to his fellow prisoners and to write encouraging letters to his family in the face of his imminent death, because he knew, deep in his heart, that nothing, "neither death, nor life, nor angels, nor rulers, nor things present, nor things to come, nor powers, nor height, nor depth, nor anything else in all creation," would be able to separate him from the love of God in Christ Jesus his Lord. (Rom.8:39)

Last Sunday after Epiphany

Hymn 136, 137   O wondrous type! O vision fair
Latin, 15th cent.; tr. *John Mason Neale (1818–1866)*

This anonymous medieval hymn was included in the Sarum breviary, the local medieval modification of the Roman rite in use at the cathedral church of Salisbury. The hymn was sung on the Feast of the Transfiguration, a celebration that inspired many hymns at the end of the fifteenth century. It is based on the story of Jesus' Transfiguration (Mt.17:1–8; Mk. 9:2–8; Lk. 9:28–36), which we celebrate on August 6. We also remember the event on the last Sunday after the Epiphany, as one of the *epiphaneia*, or divine manifestations, of Jesus.

Our English text is an adaptation of a translation by the great hymnodist John Mason Neale. Neale was educated at Trinity College, Cambridge, where, despite his Evangelical roots, he became identified with the Oxford Movement and was one of the founders of a local expression of the movement, known as the Cambridge Camden Society. After ordination, he was unable to accept a parish because of ill health, and spent the next three winters in Madeira, India.

From 1846 until his death, he was warden of Sackville College, East Grinstead, an almshouse for indigent elderly men, at a salary of £28 a year. There, he divided his time between his literary and scholarly activities and the Sisterhood of St. Margaret, which he founded in 1855. This community focused on the education of girls and the care of the sick, and though it at first met with violent opposition—even rioting—from Protestant quarters, it developed into one of the leading religious communities in the Anglican Communion.

Neale's liturgical practices led the Bishop of Chichester to prohibit his priestly duties from 1847 to 1863, but that did not deter him from expressing his commitment to the Oxford Movement. The movement's high regard for the spirituality and practice of the early Christian church was expressed in Neale's many translations of ancient Greek and Latin hymns and his paraphrases of Orthodox texts.

In lines penned during Neale's lifetime, one of his contemporaries wrote, "In his hymn-writing Dr. Neale has headed a new movement. He has attracted the Church to her oldest stores of praise as they are treasured in the Greek and Latin tongues."[28] English hymnody would never be the same again.

The text has two settings: a plainsong setting a century older than the text, and an eighteenth-century English hymn tune.

∽

In theological vocabulary, the word "type" means something slightly different from its meaning when we use it in common parlance. ("He's not my type!") It is more closely associated with the printer's use of the word—an image or model which is later imprinted on paper. Over a thousand years before the printing press, theologians used the word "type" to express a similar idea: something—or someone— in the past which foreshadows a future event or person.

Jonah, for example, is seen as a "type" of Jesus, because, just as Jonah was released from the whale's belly, so Jesus was released from the tomb. The Israelites' crossing of the Red Sea waters is a "type" of baptism, in which water is a threshold to a new life. The earliest Christian teachers, especially those in Alexandria, were fond of interpreting the Hebrew Scriptures as a foreshadowing of Christ. Medieval theologians followed suit. So did artisans, as anyone can discover who makes a close study of medieval stained glass, which often pairs stories from the Old and New Testaments.

But the writer of this hymn makes a giant leap! For no longer is something in the Hebrew Scriptures a "type" of something in the Gospels. No longer do all the "types" find their culmination in Jesus of Galilee.

Instead, in this hymn about the Transfiguration, Jesus Christ himself becomes a "type." And that "type" points the way to the future. "O wondrous type! O vision fair of glory that the Church may share. . . ." The bright light of the

Transfiguration falls right across us. And that is, indeed, an awesome thought.

Jesus is the "type" of our humanity as it was meant to be. When Peter and James and John were dazzled by the face of Jesus shining like the sun, it was a sign that we, as well, were meant to shine. When they saw his clothing become white as light, it was a sign that we also were to be wrapped in the light of Christ as in a garment.

The light may not be visible, as it was on the Mount of Transfiguration, although stories are told of people like the Russian holy man Seraphim of Sarov, whose face was said to glisten. For us, it is usually an invisible glow, which enlightens our minds as it warms our hearts. We are not likely to see it as much as feel it. But we recognize that light in the holy lives and radiant joy of this world's saints, known and unknown, who have been willing to accept God's gift of Transfiguration.

Orthodox Christians call this concept "deification" or "divinization." It doesn't mean that we become less human. It means that we become more so, because Transfiguration is everybody's destiny. And that is, of course, because He *is* our type!

Ash Wednesday

Hymn 143   The glory of these forty days
Latin, 6th cent.; tr. *Maurice F. Bell (1862–1947)*

This anonymous Lenten hymn has been found in one tenth-century manuscript and several later ones, but it is probably much older. In the breviaries of Sarum and York, it was assigned to Matins for the third Sunday in Lent.

The translator, Maurice Bell, was Vicar of St. Mark's Church, Regent's Park, London. An avid musician, he wrote about his experiences as chorister, organist, precentor, and parish priest in *The Art of Church Music* (1909).

The hymn is full of Scriptural references, beginning, of course, with reference to Jesus' forty-day fast in the wilderness after his baptism by John the Baptist (Mt.4:1–11, Mk.1:12–13, Lk.4:1–13). Jesus' wilderness fast is prefigured by the prophet Moses, who received the Ten Commandments in the Sinai desert (Ex.19 and 20). Moses was not quite "alone" in the wilderness, having already led the throng of Israelites there, but he alone was allowed to draw near to "the thick darkness where God was" on the summit of Sinai.

The wilderness images continue. Elijah, walking in the Jordanian wilderness with Elisha, was swept up to heaven by a chariot and horses of fire (2 Kings 2). The faithful visionary Daniel was thrown by a reluctant King Darius into the den of lions—a different kind of wilderness. The king, who himself spent the subsequent sleepless night fasting and praying, was "exceedingly glad" when he discovered the next morning that the prophet had survived unharmed. (Dan.6) Then there was John, the author of the Book of Revelation, thought by our Latin hymnwriter to be the same John who was Jesus' beloved disciple. In lonely exile on the island of Patmos in the Aegean Sea, John received God's "revelation" of Jesus as Messiah, and wrote an extraordinary book.

All these, the unknown author tells us, are examples for us to follow, "full oft in fast and prayer with thee," so that our spirits can be strengthened.

The German chorale, to which these words are set, expresses well the strength that comes through such discipline and prayer.

❧

The glory of these forty days we celebrate? I certainly did not "celebrate" the glory of these forty days when I was a child and dutifully "gave up" candy, ice cream, cookies, and cake during the very season in which my birthday occurred! It was a time in history when the emphasis of the church was on Lent as a season of penitence, and I considered fasting from "sweets" to be a way of demonstrating contrition.

Fasting is, of course, a powerful symbol of contrition. It can be personal contrition; it can also be contrition on behalf of others—an enacted form of prayer, such as in a hunger fast for some good cause.

But fasting can be something more, something more in tune with Lent as a celebration. It can be a means of gaining freedom. Just as the Israelites gained freedom when they crossed the Red Sea into the desert in order to escape Pharaoh, Lent can be a yearly opportunity for "Exodus," in which we practice escaping from habits that imprison us.

When you think of Lent as an opportunity for the glorious freedom of the Exodus, you realize that it is not usually food that you need to "give up." It is whatever you use to fill the emptiness that can only be filled by God. Sometimes denying ourselves these "comforting" habits— whether they be using television as a drug, or eating or drinking too much, or cramming our lives so full that we have no time for looking inward or being with our families —seems like going into the wilderness. Leaving behind the habitual consolations we have come to depend upon can be difficult. The wilderness can seem lonely and frightening.

Freedom meant that the Israelites left behind the customary foods of Egypt—the meat, the fish, the cucumbers, the melons, the leeks, the onions, and the garlic. But God sustained them with manna. And God will sustain us, once we take our own small step into the wilderness by "fasting" from whatever limits our freedom. We will be strengthened by a different kind of nourishment: our relationship with God.

We can truly celebrate that kind of Lent, because it trains us in new ways of living, not merely during the forty days, but for the rest of our lives.

First Sunday in Lent

Hymn 146, 147   Now let us all with one accord
Att. *Gregory the Great (540–604)*

This hymn is found in several tenth-century manuscripts, although it has been attributed to a great church leader four centuries earlier, Pope Gregory I. The attribution, although never proven, is in harmony with Gregory's character.

Son of a Roman senator, Gregory became prefect of the city when he was thirty-three. Shortly thereafter, he sold his vast property, gave the proceeds to the poor, and founded seven monasteries, six in Sicily and one in Rome, which he himself entered as a monk. The cloistered and austere life he chose was to last only a few years, for Pope Pelagius II soon sent him as Ambassador to Constantinople. Not long after Gregory's return from Constantinople, Pelagius died, and Gregory was elected as his successor. Gregory accepted the office only after a severe interior struggle.

Gregory's pontificate was one of strenuous activity. Italy was beset by floods, famine, pestilence, and the invasion of the Lombards, and the strength of the church was threatened by the claims of the emperor in Constantinople. Gregory confronted these evils with firmness, strength of character, gentleness, and charity.

The English historian Bede recounts that Gregory once noticed some fair-skinned Saxon slaves in the Roman market place and asked about their identity. When he was told they were Angles, he made the famous response: *Non Angli, sed angeli* ("Not Angles, but Angels"). This encounter inspired Gregory to organize an evangelizing mission to the Anglo-Saxons under Augustine, a monk from Gregory's monastery. In 597, Augustine, with a small group from his monastery, was to land in Kent and make his way to Canterbury.

Gregory fostered the development of liturgical music; his name has been so closely linked with plainsong that it is sometimes known as "Gregorian chant." He was a prolific author, noted especially for a classic treatise about the ministry entitled *Pastoral Care*. His life was characterized by a humility demonstrated in the title he took upon himself, *Servus servorum Dei* ("Servant of the servants of God"). He was canonized by popular acclamation immediately after his death.

The text of this hymn, whether it is from the pen of Gregory or not, was certainly created by a spirit very like his.

❧

"Now let us all with one accord . . . keep vigil with our heavenly Lord." Our Lenten vigil is modeled on Jesus' forty-day vigil in the wilderness after his baptism. There he was tempted to turn from his call from God and instead to seek instant fame as wonder worker and political liberator. In the Jordan, Jesus discovered who he was: God's "beloved son." In the desert, he discovered who he was not.

The first Christians prepared for Easter by undertaking a similar vigil. They discovered "who they were" and they discovered "who they did not wish to be." Converts to the faith were prepared for Holy Baptism, notorious sinners were reconciled to the fellowship of the church through penitence and forgiveness, and the whole congregation was reminded of the need for repentance and pardon. It was as if the community went together into a wilderness place where they could waken to the truth about themselves.

A vigil is a period of watchfulness. It may describe the wakeful hours spent at the bedside of a dying friend. It may describe the darkness of the bright night before Easter, with its liturgy of sacred history and Eucharist. And it certainly describes the season of Lent. During Lent we are called to be extraordinarily awake.

If you are like me, you have found that, during the times that you lie sleepless in the middle of the night, your thoughts are not as easily controlled by your conscious mind as they usually are. It is in the middle of the night that I know what is bothering me. It is in the middle of the night that physical aches I might ignore during the busy hours of the day clamor for attention. It is then that my spiritual aches also make their claim. It is in the middle of the night that I discover what I've forgotten to do. It is in the middle of the night that I discover for whom I am still grieving. It is in the middle of the night that I feel the pangs of conscience. In the middle of the night, my psychological defenses against acknowledging these things are very vulnerable.

The vigil of Lent gives us an opportunity to waken to that kind of awareness: to discover what is troubling our consciences, to discover where we need healing, to discover what one wise spiritual mentor of mine once described as "the dark corners in our hearts." These "inner demons" want us not to notice them; our temptation is to flee from this wilderness.

But we can dare to stay there, aware and honest, "in company with ages past" of Christians, and with our Lord in the wilderness. We can dare, because we know that God understands our frailty, desires our repentance, and assures us of forgiveness and healing.

Second Sunday in Lent

Hymn 448, 449   **O love, how deep, how broad, how high**
Latin, 15th cent.; tr. *Benjamin Webb (1819–1885)*

This hymn is a superb example of the texts bequeathed us by the members of the Oxford and Cambridge Camden Movements, who recovered for the church a treasure-trove of medieval texts. Its translator, Benjamin Webb, was a college friend of the great hymnodist, John Mason Neale, with whom he founded the Cambridge Camden Society.

After several curacies, Webb was eventually appointed rector of St. Andrew's, Wells Street, London, where the parish gained wide fame for the excellence of its musical services. He wrote widely about ecclesiology and hymnody and translated many ancient texts. For this hymn, Webb selected eight stanzas of a hymn written for the feast of the nativity.

Its style betrays the influence of Thomas à Kempis (1380–1471); in fact, at one time it was thought to be the work of that author. Thomas à Kempis is best known for his classic, *The Imitation of Christ*. His writings are pervaded by a spirit known as *devotio moderna* ("modern devotion"), a term applied to the revival of the spiritual life which, from the end of the fourteenth century, spread from Holland to parts of Germany, France, and Italy. It laid great stress on the inner life of the individual and encouraged methodical meditation, especially on the life and passion of Christ.

Thomas writes, "Let all the study of our heart be, therefore, from henceforth to have our meditation wholly fixed in the life and in the holy teachings of Jesus Christ."[29] This hymn puts that advice into practice by reviewing Jesus life, from his baptism to his ascension, with the subjective emphasis ("For *us* baptized, for *us* he bore. . . .") typical of *devotio moderna*. These are framed by the introductory and concluding stanzas, which well illustrate Thomas's words: "I shall sing to thee the song of love, and I shall follow Thee, my Beloved, by highness of thought, wheresoever Thou go; and my soul shall never be weary to praise Thee with the joyful song of ghostly love that I shall sing to Thee."[30]

Both tunes chosen for this text express the breadth of that "ghostly love." Hymn 448 sets the text to a strong eighteenth-century French church melody. The music for Hymn 449, contemporary with the text, is believed to have been written in the first quarter of the fifteenth century to commemorate King Henry V's victory over the French at Agincourt.

∽

"How passing thought and fantasy . . . , that God, the Son of God, should take our mortal form for mortals' sake."

"For God so loved the world that he gave his only Son, that whoever believes in him should not perish . . . ." (Jn. 3:16)

We Christians, especially those of us who have listened to the stories of Jesus from childhood, often do not realize what a shocking—even unthinkable—event the Incarnation was. We have, most of us, grown to take it for granted that the Son of God "took mortal form for mortals' sake." It is too easy to sing this hymn without feeling the impact of the scandalous belief that Jesus walked through the events of his life "for us."

We perhaps need to make an imaginary leap, and ask ourselves, "What if we had never heard of him?"

Our small friend Evie never had. She was a child crippled by muscular dystrophy, confined to a wheelchair. Her father, a cantor in a synagogue near our home, also sang in New York City as a free-lance baritone in various concert halls and churches. Evie often was taken by her parents to hear him rehearse and perform.

At one point, Evie began talking about what her parents thought was an imaginary friend, a fantasy. She called her friend "the Broken Man." Somehow, the "Broken Man" consoled her about her disability in a way that nothing had before.

One day, the family took Evie to hear her father sing in Riverside Church, the great church that stands on the shore of the Hudson in New York's Morningside Heights. As they were wheeling Evie out of the church, she suddenly became very excited: "There's the Broken Man! There's the Broken Man!"

They followed her gaze. High on the wall was a crucifix. And there, hanging on the crucifix was the Broken Man. He was the first friend Evie had ever found who took her mortal form, so that children like her would know that God cared about brokenness. He was not imaginary, after all.

Evie's parents, pious Jews, did not forget what the Broken Man had given their daughter. Their love for Evie mirrored God's love, so deep, so broad, so high. They gave her a book, *The Greatest Story Ever Told*, with a picture of the crucified Jesus on the bright red cover. And every Christmas they placed a small Christmas tree in the corner of the playroom and framed her bedroom window with colored lights. The Broken Man brought Evie comfort until the day she died, just a few short years later.

Third Sunday in Lent

Hymn 148   **Creator of the earth and skies**
Donald W. Hughes (1911–1967)

Donald Hughes was born in Lancashire, England, and educated at Emmanuel College, Cambridge. He taught at The Leys School, Cambridge from 1934 to 1946, and then became headmaster at Rydal School, a residential school in North Wales founded by the English Methodists. It was there that he began to use his exceptional gifts for hymn-writing. "Creator of the earth and skies" appeared in *Hymns for Church and School* in 1964, although most of his hymns were still in manuscript when he died an untimely death in a car accident.

Erik Routley writes about "Creator of the earth and skies": "Hughes has . . . produced a perfect lyric, serious but hopeful, not a word out of place, with a Wesley-like balance between the massive words and the small ones."[31]

This strong hymn reflects the time of history through which the author lived. Although he was only in early childhood during the First World War, he would have been aware of adult conversations about the ravages and losses of war. He was in his mid-twenties during the rise of Hitler, thirty during the Battle of Britain, and thirty-four when the atomic bomb fell on Hiroshima. No wonder that he wrote "the wreckage of our hatred spreads."

☙

When I was a teenager, my priest gave me a small black book which included a list of questions to be used in self-examination before confession. These questions were grouped under the headings of "pride," "idolatry," "profanity," "irreverence," "disobedience," "hate," "impurity," "theft," "deceit," and "discontent." They were, I realize, an elaboration of the spirit of the Ten Commandments in terms which helped me to look back over my behavior periodically. This little book was like a "primer," a first book which taught me how to *behave* in such a way that I could assure myself that I was following the way of the God of Love.

That isn't so easy anymore.

One of the privileges—and the difficulties—of growing older is that one's vision widens. I know now that, even if I were to win the struggle against the personal, individual sins in the small black book, I contribute to "sin" in a more serious sense. For the most part, I cannot avoid doing this. The "sin" is a product of living at the time I am living, in the place I am living, in the style I am living.

Take our car, for example. If I need to travel farther than my bicycle will take me, I use our car. Our car consumes a fossil fuel, an assured supply of which has caused our country to make certain foreign policy decisions which have involved the killing of innocent civilians. Our car, no matter how well we maintain it, emits fumes which eventually will contribute to global warming.

Or take coffee. Until recently, if I wanted coffee, I have only been able to buy brands raised on huge plantations that have claimed land that once was rain forest. Depleting the rainforest contributes to the ill-health of the atmosphere; it also contributes to the extinction of thousands of species of animal and plant life. The people who work on these planta-tions get paid minimally for their work; the profit goes to the large corporations who own them.

I could continue. Our family's taxes pay for weapons of mass destruction. I live in a state which retains the death penalty. The computer on which I am writing cannot be recycled and will end up in a landfill. I am well fed while others starve, live in a house while others are homeless, and have access to health care while others have no medicines.

I find myself overwhelmed when I think of sin. It is no longer sufficient to look at the list in the small black book. There are graver sins of which society as a whole is guilty, sins against the Creator of earth and skies. And I am part of that society.

What can I do? I can ask for God's *truth* to "make me wise," trying to live in such a way that my life does not damage any other life—whether the life of air, water, flora, fauna, or other human beings. And I can ask for God's power to "make me strong" in resisting the forces of evil. Most of all, I can come to God in penitence, and ask God to help me live and act courageously, to help turn our earth's "darkness into day."

Fourth Sunday in Lent

Hymn 465, 466   Eternal light, shine in my heart
Christopher Idle (b.1938); from a prayer of Alcuin (735?–804)

Alcuin was born into a noble family near York and was educated at the cathedral school there, where he inherited the traditions and zeal of the early English church. He eventually became head of the school and was ordained as a deacon. In 781, he went to Italy to meet with the Emperor Charlemagne, who persuaded Alcuin to become his adviser in religious and cultural matters. As royal tutor at Aachen, he established a palace library. When Alcuin became Abbot of Tours in 796, he set up an important school and library there as well. A man of vast learning, personal charm, and integrity of character, Alcuin was largely responsible for helping to preserve the classical heritage of western civilization "in a rude and barbarous age."[32]

The contemporary British priest-poet, Christopher Idle, adapted this prayer by Alcuin in 1977 at Limehouse Rectory in inner London, where he then lived. A graduate of St. Peter's College, Oxford, Idle was ordained to the ministry of the Church of England in 1965 and soon thereafter wrote his first published hymn texts. "Eternal light" was suggested by a brief prayer of Alcuin included in *Daily Prayer*, a collection which Idle often used as a source of prayers in leading public worship.

The phrase "costly grace," in the final stanza, is taken from Dietrich Bonhoeffer's book *The Cost of Discipleship*, first published in Germany in 1937. In the first chapter, the author compares "costly grace" and "cheap grace":

> Cheap grace is the deadly enemy of our Church. We are fighting today for costly grace. [Cheap grace means] grace as a doctrine, a principle, a system. . . . the justification of sin without the justification of the sinner. . . . the preaching of forgiveness without requiring repentance. . . . grace without discipleship, grace without the cross, grace without Jesus Christ, living and incarnate.
>
> [Costly grace, continues Bonhoeffer, is] the gospel which must be *sought* again and again, the gift which must be *asked* for, the door at which a man must *knock*. Such grace is *costly* because it calls us to follow, and it is *grace* because it calls us to follow *Jesus Christ*. It is costly because it costs a man his life, and it is grace because it gives a man the only true life. It is costly because it condemns sin, and grace because it justifies the sinner. Above all, it is *costly* because it cost God the life of his Son . . . and what has cost God much cannot be cheap for us.[33]

Both tunes provided are meditative settings of the text.

☙

When I hear the words "eternal light," I always think of my little brother, who had a talent for delightful malapropisms, exclaiming, after a trip to the battlefield at Gettysburg, that he had "seen the internal light."

My brother was not too far off the mark. The eternal light at Gettysburg burned in order to kindle a similar light in the memories of Americans, as they held within their hearts all those who died in a terrible war.

The eternal qualities of which Alcuin wrote are not visible, but deeply internal. The process of discovering these qualities is a lifelong task.

When we are young, we are likely to depend on other people for these qualities. Listen to the Broadway love songs of the forties and fifties, if you want to get an idea of what it feels like to find light, hope, and life in another human being! Try to remember how it felt to break up with your first boyfriend or girlfriend, if you want proof that external light is ephemeral. It is the same with our search for power or wisdom. It is a natural part of growing up to be empowered by our favorite heroes, and edified by our wise teachers.

As we move towards our middle years, we are often urged by the voices in our culture to depend only on ourselves for the qualities we seek. You can discover that by looking at the appropriately labeled "self-help" section in any bookstore. In mid-life, we try to make our own the light, hope, power, and wisdom we seek. But what happens when we fail to find them, or, having found these qualities, find that they are failing us?

We reach true maturity when we realize that the Source of these qualities lies beyond us, and when we acknowledge our dependence on that Source. If you have had the privilege of knowing some truly holy people who are on the threshold of death, you will understand what this means.

I will never forget Mary, a faithful parishioner in a

church I served, during her last days under hospice care. The day before she died, I spent the afternoon at her bedside with a couple of members of her family. She spoke to us of her gratitude for life and recited a litany of the people for whom she was thankful. She spoke of her hope for her parish church, and prayed that God would guide it in the search for a new rector. She told us that we should not be sad, that she was going to be with the Lord, and that she was not afraid. Even in the process of dying, she retained her sense of humor: "This is taking a longer time than I thought it would!"

Mary's internal light, hope, power, and wisdom shone through that frail body. Those qualities were the result of a lifetime of practicing her dependence on the "costly" grace of a God who suffered and died for her. That grace did not let her down now. It was her "eternal light," and because it was of God, it illuminated her way to eternal life.

Fifth Sunday in Lent

Hymn 151   From deepest woe I cry to thee
Martin Luther (1483–1546); tr. *Catherine Winkworth (1827–1878)*

The hymnologist Erik Routley writes that "the success of any movement in culture or religion requires at least two people: the one who thought of it and the one who made it stick."[34] Although the Reformation had been brewing for at least 150 years before Martin Luther, it was Luther's peculiar genius to "make the Reformation stick." Many of his reforms stemmed from the belief that all Christians should be treated by the church as adult participants in worship. Luther accomplished much of this through the power of language. He wrote a German Catechism and translated a Bible that is the foundation of the modern German language. In addition, out of his concern for the people's participation in the liturgy, Luther created a uniquely German hymnody: "It is my intention to make German psalms for the people, spiritual songs whereby the word of God may be kept alive in them by singing."[35]

This paraphrase of Psalm 130 ("Out of the depths have I called you, O LORD; LORD, hear my voice"), dating from 1523, was one of the first congregational songs that Luther wrote. During that year, he also suggested that various friends and colleagues join him in writing hymns based on the psalms. Luther himself was to produce thirty-seven hymns and paraphrases. Winfred Douglas writes of the latter: "Even his paraphrases of parts of Holy Scripture were so free, so poetically powerful in the idiom of the people, that they are really new creations."[36]

Aus tiefer Not schrei ich zu dir ("From deepest woe I cry to thee") quickly became a hymn sung at German Lutheran funerals. It was used in May 1525, at the burial of the Saxon duke, Frederick the Wise, and sung again at Luther's own funeral in 1546. The chorale melody provides a moving example of word-painting; notice the falling and rising interval of a fifth on "from deepest woe."

The hymn was translated into English by Catherine Winkworth, an early pioneer of women's educational rights, who herself was educated privately in Manchester, England, and Dresden, Germany. Her splendid translations of about 400 German hymns are found in two volumes: *Lyra Germanica* (1855) and *The Chorale Book for England* (1863).

For this latter project she retranslated many of the texts in the meter of the originals so that they could be sung to their associated German melodies.

೨

"Out of the depths have I called you, O LORD; LORD, hear my voice" was a psalm Martin Luther would have prayed many times in his life as a Roman Catholic theologian, Augustinian canon, and priest. Someone with Luther's keen intelligence and passionate moral sense would probably have been in the "depths" often, as he measured himself against the holiness of God and the demands of the Christian way.

I wonder if praying this psalm of lament and trust was among the ingredients which fueled his growing feeling of alienation from Rome. The affirmation that "with the Lord there is mercy" must have helped to kindle his passionate reaction against the legalism of a church which had taught Luther that he could buy—or work—his way out of the depths, and thereby justify himself before God. When Luther finally arrived at his doctrine of "justification by faith," it was, perhaps, nothing new. He was returning to what he had known all along through Scripture, a return to the heart of what he had been praying in Psalm 130.

In that psalm, the despairing soul eagerly calls to a God who loves and understands him. He doesn't say, "I promise I will do better, so you'll save me from these depths." He doesn't say, "These depths are a just punishment for my sins." Instead, he trusts in God's forgiveness, mercy, and plenteous redemption.

Many of the people whom I have counseled during my ministry have grown up in a background of legalism like that which typified the Roman Catholic Church of Martin

Luther's time. Their experience of legalism may not have had a religious guise. But it had to do with the need to please someone, or to measure up to certain standards, in order to feel valuable as a human being.

That belief may have come from parents who were hypercritical and demanded that their child be something or someone he or she could not be. The belief may have come from a subtle inner perfectionism, a legalism created by one's own self—often a particular burden of the very intelligent. Or it may have come from a religious outlook in which human sinfulness is understood as worthlessness.

Whatever its origin, the result can be a sense of despair at ever gaining acceptance from God.

Psalm 130—and Luther's hymn—show us another way of looking at our "deepest woe," either when events befall us that diminish us or when we look at our shortcomings in the light of a righteous God.

We are not called to ignore the fact that we are in the depths. Instead, we use the reverberation of those depths— like the amplification in an immense cave—to call out with all our heart to God. We call out, knowing that the one who hears is a God who understands these turbulent, rebellious, or depressed psyches of ours better than we ourselves, because it is God who imagined the human race into being.

Our call to God is our response to God's call to *us*. Like Jesus crying to the entombed Lazarus, "Come out," God calls us to walk eagerly towards the light of divine love. That love does not demand that we prove ourselves—only that we let God unbind us, and free us from our need to be deserving.

The Sunday of the Passion: Palm Sunday

Hymn 156   Ride on! ride on in majesty!
Henry Hart Milman (1791–1868)

Henry Hart Milman was the son of the physician to George III. He received his education at Eton and at Brasenose College in Oxford, where he was awarded prizes for his poetry, and where Reginald Heber was among his close friends. After ordination, he spent three years as vicar of St. Mary's, Reading, but he left parish ministry when he was appointed professor of poetry at Oxford. He introduced German biblical-critical techniques of historical research in his *History of the Jews*, the "first English book to . . . use the Bible as an historical source-book without denying its special status as revelation."[37] In 1835, he became rector of St. Margaret's, London, and canon of Westminster, and continued there until he was made dean of St. Paul's Cathedral in 1849. He died in London in 1868 and was buried in St. Paul's.

Milman's hymn about Jesus' entry into Jerusalem (Mt.21:1–9; Mk.11:1–10; Lk.19:28–38; Jn:12:12–16) first appeared in his friend Reginald Heber's posthumous *Hymns written and adapted to the Weekly Church Service of the Year*. It is said that when Heber received the manuscript of "Ride on" for the collection in which he was trying to include the work of the best living poets, he exclaimed, "A few more hymns like this, and I need not wait for the help of Scott and Southey!"[38] The text also appeared in Milman's own *Selection of Psalms and Hymns* (1837).

"Ride on! ride on in majesty!" is thought to be one of the finest hymns in the English language. Lionel Adey writes, "Blending lucidity and highly conscious art, [Milman's] 'Ride on, ride on in majesty' yields to no hymn in English in its appeal to the whole range of human intelligence and sensitivity."[39] Hymnologist Carol Doran points out that there are no less than twenty-two exclamation marks in this hymn, conveying "a sense of resolute courage in the face of unavoidable tragedy."[40]

The solemn unison tune in *The Hymnal 1982* was composed in 1939 by the Canadian composer Graham George, who wrote:

> It originated as a result of a choir practice before Palm Sunday . . . during which I had been thinking WINCHESTER NEW is a fine tune, but it has nothing whatever to do with the tragic trumpets, as one might theatrically call them, of Palm Sunday. At breakfast the following morning I was enjoying my toast and marmalade when the first two lines of this tune sang themselves unbidden into my mind. This seemed too good to miss, so I went to my study, allowed the half-tune to complete itself—which it did with very little trouble—and there it was.[41]

ॐ

When I was a teenager, our parish youth group would gather during the week before Palm Sunday for an annual project. We would take some of the long palm fronds ordered from some distant land by the Altar Guild, and fold them in such a way that, by the end of our meeting, there was a basket full of palm crosses ready to be given to the congregation on Palm Sunday. It was a sociable time, full of adolescent chatter. Some of the boys would inevitably duel with one another before folding their palms, while the girls kept at our task, despite the fact that our hands would begin to sting from working with the knife-edged fronds.

During that liturgical era in the church, Palm Sunday was a celebratory day. People who came to church on Christmas and Easter would also come on Palm Sunday to "get their palms," which then would be dutifully tucked behind a picture in their bedrooms. We young people liked it because it was a day for processions with rousing hymns. While the palm crosses we had made during our lively youth group meeting gave a hint of the Passion to come, we didn't think much about that. Nor did we really notice all the words of a hymn like "Ride on! ride on in majesty!" On one level, we knew what was to come: Holy Week, with Good Friday at the end. But we didn't think about it much on Palm Sunday. Palm Sunday was the day for parades.

When Good Friday came, with Holy Saturday and Easter on its heels, there would be much talk about the spiritual passage from death to resurrection, and its connection to the events in our lives. But there was never much talk about the other kind of spiritual passage—the passage which occurred between the Entry into Jerusalem and the Garden of Gethsemane, the passage from triumph into desolation.

One of my teachers once said that there is nothing that happens to us that did not happen to Jesus. We have Jesus' companionship in all our life's events, joyous and desolate.

I think we are fortunate in our Palm Sunday liturgy to be able to practice walking with Jesus along the road into Jerusalem, pursuing his path until it reaches the Garden of

Gethsemane and the Hill of Golgotha. When we walk that path with him, we will be able to understand more easily that Jesus walks with us, as we ourselves move through the passages from apparent triumph to apparent failure. For that is an inevitable pattern in life.

Who has not known that plunge? Perhaps we love our job and think we are doing good work, and are told one day that we are no longer needed. Perhaps we have given our hearts in love to someone, and discover that they do not love us any more. Perhaps we have trusted someone, and are betrayed. Perhaps we think we are in the bloom of health, and suddenly get bad news from the doctor.

Jesus chose to walk this difficult path with us. He "emptied himself, taking the form of a servant, being born in the likeness of men. And being found in human form he humbled himself and became obedient unto death, even death on a cross." (Phil.2:7–8)

We do not need to wait until Easter to hear good news. We, who need the companionship of Jesus during our own passages from triumph to desolation, already recognize good news on Palm Sunday!

Monday in Holy Week

Hymn 164   **Alone thou goest forth, O Lord**
Peter Abelard (1079–1142); tr. *F. Bland Tucker (1895–1984)*

Peter Abelard, the eldest son of a noble Breton family, showed evidence of his lively and independent mind while he was still a youth. He became a canon at the Cathedral of Notre Dame in Paris, where his lectures on theology and dialectics, noted for their clarity, brought him many students. While at Notre Dame, he fell in love with Héloise, niece of another canon by the name of Fulbert. The pair eventually fled to Brittany, where they were privately married and a son was born to them.

On their return to Paris, Canon Fulbert hired men to emasculate Abelard. Héloise then took the veil and Abelard became a monk, remaining for a short period in solitude at the Abbey of St. Denis. But Abelard's lively mind could not let him long resist the vocation of teaching, and when he began to lecture once again, crowds thronged to hear him.

Attacks began to be made on Abelard's orthodoxy. St. Bernard of Clairvaux instituted a trial for heresy based on Abelard's *Theologia*; Abelard was found guilty and was forced to cease teaching.

Abelard and Héloise are buried together in the Cemetery of Pere-la-Chaise, Paris. Their romance has been made into a number of novels and plays, and their letters have been published in many languages.

Solus ad victimam procedis, Domine is from a collection of meditative poems, the *Hymnaris Paraclitensis* that Abelard wrote for his wife Héloïse's Convent of the Paraclete. This deeply moving meditation on the solitary figure of Jesus at "earth's darkest hour," was appointed for the third nocturnal office on Good Friday.

F. Bland Tucker's free translation was written in 1938.

The music is a somber minor chorale that suggests the heavy footsteps of One bearing the burden, not only of a cross, but of the world's sins.

↰↱

Abelard's exquisite Passiontide hymn suggests the paradox and mystery of suffering, in particular the suffering of the Son of God on Good Friday—earth's "darkest hour." We who know Abelard's story realize that he was intimately acquainted with suffering—that he also was obliged to go forth alone, after the dissolution of his family and enforced estrangement from his teaching and theological vocation.

And yet he finds himself able to write, "Grant us with thee to suffer pain."

Those words tell us that, when we walk the Way of the Cross in our prayer—from the praetorium of Pontius Pilate to the hill of Golgotha—we eventually reach Jesus' "joy and resurrection power."

But I think that they mean something much more profound, as well.

They surely meant something more to Abelard. We can guess that Abelard had discovered that those two small words, "with thee" transformed his own suffering. When his own physical, spiritual, and emotional pain seemed like an insupportable burden, those two small words "with thee" placed Abelard's pain on the Cross of redemption. That gesture in the midst of his suffering made it possible to go on.

Second Isaiah wrote about a mysterious figure, identified by Biblical scholars as the "suffering servant." The suffering servant was chosen by God; God delighted in him. Yet he bore the infirmities of his people; he was stricken and "wounded for our transgressions." (Isa.53:4–5)

Students of the Bible still discuss the identity of this figure; was he an individual, or a symbol for the exiled Hebrew nation? For Christians, one thing is certain, Jesus would have been familiar with the figure of the suffering servant. And it is upon him that the mysterious mantle of the servant fell on Good Friday.

Jesus suffered. And God suffers. Jesus, the suffering servant, reminds us that God suffers.

The suffering servant figure tells us that our own suffering need not diminish us, but that it can become redemptive. We need only offer our suffering to God as if it were a prayer. The Russian spiritual writer, Catherine de Hueck Doherty, writes:

> Sorrow is a state of union with God in the pain of men. It is a state of deep and profound understanding. It is as if God put his hand out and the panorama of the whole world and its pain is opened before you. This is the action of the Holy Spirit. The gift of tears flows. . . . Afterwards I don't know why I cried or what started or stopped it. But I know that it came from God. Something happened in the world that made God cry and he invited me to cry. Or perhaps I cried and invited him to cry.[42]

When we place our sufferings on the Cross, we are no longer alone. When we allow ourselves to open our hearts to the world's suffering, our pain becomes prayer, and our tears become part of the redemptive work of a suffering God.

Tuesday in Holy Week

Hymn 165, 166   Sing, my tongue, the glorious battle
Venantius Honorius Fortunatus (540?–600?); tr. *John Mason Neale (1818–1866)*

Venantius Honorius Fortunatus, born near Treviso in northern Italy, was converted to Christianity at an early age, and educated in rhetoric, grammar and law at Ravenna, then under Byzantine rule. When Fortunatus developed a severe eye disease which threatened blindness, he is said to have recovered his sight after anointing his eyes with oil from a lamp burning before the altar of St. Martin of Tours in Ravenna. In thanksgiving for his recovery, he set out on a pilgrimage to St. Martin's shrine in Tours. He was to spend most of the rest of his adult life in Gaul.

There, he was soon to meet the Frankish Queen Rhade-gonda, who had been captured in battle and forced to wed the Frankish King Clotaire I. Eventually separating from her husband, she founded an abbey at Poitiers; an avid collector of relics, she secured from Justin II, the Byzantine emperor, a relic of the True Cross for the abbey. She named her abbey Sainte Croix, in honor of this gift from Constantinople.

She and Fortunatus became friends, and she persuaded him to take holy orders and to enter the abbey. Fortunatus was to became Bishop of Poitiers in 599, not long before his death.

During his lifetime, Fortunatus produced numerous

poetic writings, ranging from rhymes thanking his hosts for dinner to some of the finest poetry in Christendom.

It is thought that "Sing, my tongue, the glorious battle" was written for the procession which carried Queen Rhadegonda's relic of the True Cross to Poitiers on November 19, 569. Another hymn, *Vexilla regis prodeunt*—"The royal banners forward go"—was probably written for the same occasion.

"Sing, my tongue, the glorious battle," one of the finest hymns of the Middle Ages, was sung by the Crusaders on their way to the Holy Land. One can almost hear the marching of the Christian legions to its rhythm:

> *Pange, lingua, gloriosi*
> *Proelium certaminis,*
> *Et super Crucis tropaeo*
> *Dic triumphum nobilem:*
> *Qualiter Redemptor orbis*
> *Immolatus vicerit.*

༄

I have just returned from visiting an exhibition of art treasures from the Vatican collections. In the middle of the first gallery is a solitary reliquary, considered the most important object in the treasury of St. Peter's basilica. It is the Cross of Justin II, given by the Byzantine emperor to the Roman pope sometime between 565 and 578. One cannot help but imagine that this same emperor's gift to Queen Rhadagonda's abbey in Poitiers must have looked something like this.

The silver and gold Cross of Justin II is set with large and small gems of many shapes and colors. They surround an inscription in Latin: Ligno Quo Christus Humanum

Subdidit Hostem ("The wood where the human Christ was placed by his Enemy") Dat Romae Iustinus Opem et Socia Decorem ("Justin and his wife gave Rome this beautiful work"). In the very center of this amazing object, a small glass window reveals a few fragments of wood, wood believed to be splinters from the True Cross.

I never really understood reliquaries until my husband found, among his deceased mother's possessions, a yellowed envelope on which was written "flower from a wreath of Beethoven's funeral flowers on his piano." Awed, we gathered up the dried petals that fell out, realizing that it was, indeed, quite probable that his mother, a musician born in 1887, had been given the flower by a friend whose own mother had been alive at the time of Beethoven's death. There was something about touching something that was so closely connected with genius that made us want to treasure those flowers. We asked an artist friend to make a twentieth-century version of a reliquary: a collage incorporating the envelope and the petals, which now hangs in our violinist son's apartment.

Now, it is not surprising to me that artistry was lavished on a fragment of the Cross.

Nor does the juxtaposition of the worldly splendor of Byzantine materials and craftsmanship and the plainness of the small bits of wood encased in the center offend me. It serves to remind me, during this Holy Week, of a typically Orthodox perspective on the crucifixion: that the crucifixion was a cosmic battle against evil in which Christ triumphed. As I contemplate Jesus' death on the Cross, that perspective enhances my understanding of the paradox of the suffering of the Son of God.

The bejeweled reliquary reminds me that the battle waged on Golgotha was a glorious one. All of the thirty years Jesus lived among us pointed toward this moment of battle against the power of darkness—the moment of the nails, the spitting, the vinegar, the spear, and the reed. His broken body was at the exact center of a cosmic moment, in which not only humanity, but earth, stars, sky and ocean were freed from bondage to evil. The "sweet weight" which hung on that tree was the body of *Christus Victor*: the victorious Christ.

It is no wonder that a poet educated at Ravenna in the Byzantine tradition venerated such a cross: "sweetest wood, and sweetest iron!"—a noble tree that cradled the sweet weight of the victorious Christ in its arms, as a mother cradles her child.

This cross had mothered not a defeat, but a victory. The creator of the Cross of Justin II which was sent to Rome—and of that other reliquary which was sent to Poitiers—expressed his gratitude for that victory by surrounding a few rough splinters of wood with dazzling beauty. Fortunatus expressed his gratitude for that victory through the heart-wrenching images of his poetry. How do we express our gratitude for the victory of that "sweetest weight" hung on a noble tree?

Wednesday in Holy Week

Hymn 163   **Sunset to sunrise changes now**
Clement of Alexandria (170?–220?); para. *Howard Chandler Robbins (1876–1952)*

Clement, probably an Athenian by birth, was a cultured philosopher who sought the truth in many schools of thought until he met the Christian philosopher Pantaenus, the head of the Catechetical School at Alexandria. Alexandria in the second century was a thriving center of intellectual inquiry, housing a great library containing a superb collection of the world's literature. All of the philosophical systems had "schools" there: the Platonists, Neo-Platonists, Stoics, Epicureans, Cynics, and the cults of the Mystery Religions. By the second century, the city had become a focal point for Gnosticism, a comprehensive term for several theories of salvation which emphasized the Christian's "Gnosis" or secret and esoteric knowledge accessible only to a few. Gnosticism was considered a heresy by the church authorities.

Clement asserted that there was a true Christian Gnosis, which could be found in the Scriptures and was available to all. He taught that Greek philosophy was not inconsistent with Christianity but a handmaid to it, preparing the Greeks for the coming of the Logos, or God's Word incarnate. Eventually Clement succeeded Pantaenus as head of the Catechetical School, and his teaching helped to commend Christianity to the intellectual circles of Alexandria and to prepare the way for his pupil Origen, the most eminent theologian of early Greek Christianity.

During the persecutions under the Emperor Severus in 202, Clement fled Alexandria to go into exile in Jerusalem. In 211, Alexander, bishop of Jerusalem, wrote to Antioch commending Clement as "a blessed presbyter who had strengthened the Church of Jerusalem." Four years later, he wrote to Origen, mentioning "holy Clement, one of those blessed fathers who have gone on before us."[43]

Clement has sometimes been called the first Christian hymnwriter, for he wrote original hymns based neither on the psalms nor on New Testament canticles. He once described himself and his fellow Christians thus: "We plough the fields praising; we sail the seas hymning."[44]

Clement's *Protrepticus*, the source of "Sunset to sunrise changes now," is one of the few evangelistic tracts left from ancient times. The hymn, contained in a chapter on the mystery of Christ's death, was translated and quoted in the 1938 Bohlen Lectures by General Theological Seminary professor of pastoral theology, Howard Chandler Robbins. The following year, he published the paraphrase in his book, *Preaching the Gospel*.

The setting of Clement's text is a melody from the American folk collection *Southern Harmony*.

എ

Among all the poetry or art inspired by Jesus' crucifixion, Clement of Alexandria's "Sunset to sunrise" perhaps most perfectly illustrates the theology of Alexandrian Christianity. This is a crucifixion that illuminates. The illumination that brings a wondrous dawn to the world, transforming sunset to sunrise, emanates from the thorn-crowned brow of the Savior. The sacred head has become a heavenly lamp, lighting humanity's way to eternity.

Clement had a high regard for the mind. He understood God's Logos, or Word, as the source of human reason. He saw ignorance and error as a fundamental evil.

At first glance, we might not agree with him. But when we look at where ignorance has brought us in our time, we wonder if Clement was not right. Cannot deliberate ignorance be just as wrong as intentional sin?

This is perhaps most obvious today in the matters of environmental stewardship which should be of concern to the church. If we are serious about caring for creation, one of the first things we must do is to learn. For this is a relatively new science; when I was a college student, "environmental studies" was unheard of. The result of our communal ignorance is that we make sinful decisions about our transportation, buildings, businesses, and lifestyles.

But we don't know it. Ignorance may be bliss for us, but it is not for other parts of creation. Our ignorance pollutes rivers, air, and land, and brings many species to the point of extinction. Ignorance may be bliss today, but it will not be bliss tomorrow, for our children, grandchildren, and great-grandchildren. Our ignorance today threatens to create a crowded, toxic world in which nobody will want to live.

Or take ignorance about injustices against other human beings. Was it not a sin to fail to acknowledge what Hitler really was doing? Would God want us to prefer not to know the painful facts about the incarceration and torture of innocent human beings in our own day?

Clement would probably tell us that mental darkness is a weapon of the Prince of Darkness, and that the "blinders" we so comfortably don are as evil as deliberate, active sinning.

We need to pray that the light from Christ's brow will illuminate our own brows—not just our hearts. We need to ask God to illuminate our minds, in this complex world in which there is ever more to learn about how to be a responsible and faithful Christian. We need to recognize that the issues which face us today require thought, even serious study.

We need to realize that reason and grace do not conflict, that knowledge and faith are a winning combination. And, finally, we need to pray that Christ's light will continue to dawn on the church and on us, the *homo sapiens*—thinking people—who sing its hymns.

Maundy Thursday

Hymn 602   Jesu, Jesu, fill us with your love
Ghanaian, tr. Thomas Stevenson Colvin (b.1925)

Born in Glasgow and educated at Glasgow University's Trinity College, Thomas Stevenson Colvin was originally trained and employed as an engineer. He left his position with the Royal Indian Engineers for the ministry of the Church of Scotland and was ordained in 1954. His service in Africa, first as missionary in Malawi and Northern Ghana, and then as Development Advisor to the Central African Synod, spanned the years from 1959 to 1974. During those years he encouraged native peoples to compose their own hymn texts, which were sung to traditional folk melodies. He helped fill the need for "basic hymns in simple English which could also be translated into local languages"[45] He privately published some of these hymns in two collections, *Free to Serve* (1968) and *Leap my Soul* (1976). The Hope Publishing

Company published another collection, *Fill Us With Your Love*, in 1983.

Colvin writes that he translated "Jesu, Jesu" for the people "in newly planted village churches in the multi-language districts around Tamale."[46] He also describes the way it would have been sung: worshipers would perform it in "our own way, with the overlap of voices, the addition of harmonies and the use of percussion and rhythms."[47]

Colvin is now a member of the Iona Community, an ecumenical community of men and women seeking new ways of living the Gospel in today's world. Although the community is based on the island of Iona off the coast of Scotland and in a central office in Glasgow, its approximately 200 members and 900 associates live throughout the world, joining in the common work for justice and peace. Colvin has returned to Africa, "serving the neighbors he has from Jesu" as a participant in the Christian Council of Malawi's refugee work.

The text of "Jesu, Jesu" is inspired by the story of Jesus washing the disciples' feet at the Last Supper from the Gospel of John (Jn.13:1–15): "Jesus . . . rose from supper, laid aside his garments, and girded himself with a towel. Then he poured water into a basin, and began to wash the disciples' feet, and to wipe them with the towel with which he was girded."

After Simon Peter's anguished refusal and subsequent acquiescence to Jesus' humble ministry, Jesus reminds his disciples, "If I then, your Lord and Teacher, have washed your feet, you also ought to wash one another's feet. For I have given you an example, that you also should do as I have done to you."

❧

One of the guidelines for meditating on Scripture is to pay particular attention to a word or phrase that "jumps out at you," asking for your attention.

There is a phrase that does just that to me in "Jesu, Jesu, fill us with your love." It is the phrase, "serving as though we were slaves."

Considering the African origin of "Jesu, Jesu," I have always found the use of the word "slaves" shocking to the point of being offensive. Surely that was a loaded word for Thomas Colvin's African friends.

The slave is property—owned by someone else—with no choice about his or her work. I recoil at the thought.

And then the words of some of my spiritual forbears begin to well up in my memory, to help me understand "serving as though we were slaves."

I remember St. Paul: "Or do you not know that your body is a temple of the Holy Spirit within you, which you have from God, and that you are not your own? For you were bought with a price; therefore glorify God in your body." (1 Cor.6:19–20)

The truth is that we are "owned"; in our heart of hearts, we are so connected to our Creator that the only way we can talk about it adequately is to say we "belong" to God. We can run away from God; we can refuse to acknowledge our "owner"; we can disobey. But, deep in our psyches, there is a longing to return. St. Augustine of Hippo, three centuries later, would express it this way: "You have made us for Yourself, and our hearts are restless 'til they rest in You." When I fret about the concept of being "owned," Paul and Augustine remind me that we have been bought already. The currency used was not gold or silver but the creative, sacrificial, inexhaustible love of God.

When I balk at the idea of being without choice in my work, I think of Teresa of Avila, the great Counter-Reformation saint, who writes of a time when the Lord "told her that it was time she took upon her His affairs as if they were her own and that He would take her affairs upon Himself."[48] Teresa had reached a spiritual state in which her free will was so in tune with God's will that she did not any longer have to make decisions about ministry. It was as if she had no choice but to do the work of her Lord.

When Christians gather to re-enact the Footwashing, we are practicing what Teresa knew: a ministry guided effortlessly by the impetus of Love.

Many people would prefer being the foot-washers, rather than the recipients of that ministry. So on Maundy Thursday, when we allow another to wash our feet, we also practice receiving the ministry of that love.

We find that currency showered upon us, if we look around us at God's abundant world and remember what God has done for us through our Lord and Master. And we may finally recognize the paradox that this kind of slavery is the passport to freedom: the freedom of knowing who we are—God's own—and what will bring us joy—God's work.

Good Friday

Hymn 168, 169   O sacred head, sore wounded

Paul Gerhardt (1607–1676); tr. *Robert Seymour Bridges
(1844–1930)* and *J. W. Alexander (1804–1859)*

The career of the beloved German hymnwriter Paul Gerhardt
was delayed by the Thirty Years War and by poverty. Finally,
at the age of forty-five, he was offered a parish in a small
village, was married to the woman he had long loved, and
began to publish the hymns he had for many years been
writing. The hymns brought him fame and opportunity.
When he was called in 1657 as assistant pastor to the great St.
Nikolaikirche in Berlin, he became known as a fine preacher
and a man of deep piety and good works. However, in 1666,
he resigned this post through unwillingness to assent to an
edict of the Elector of Brandenburg which forbade free
discussion of the differences between the Lutheran and the
Reformed Churches. Two years later, he was appointed as
archdeacon at Lubben, where he remained until his death.

Although he was theologically a staunch Lutheran, Gerhardt was influenced by Catholic mysticism, especially that
of the school of St. Bernard of Clairvaux. "O sacred head,
sore wounded" is based on a Latin text, traditionally attributed to Bernard, but possibly written by Arnulf of Louvain
(1200–1250).

The hymn is a free translation of the final part of a poem
of seven parts, to be sung on different days of the week.
Captioned a "rhythmical prayer to the various members of
Christ's body suffering and hanging on the Cross," the poem

addresses in turn Jesus' feet, knees, hands, sides, breast, heart, and head. Whether or not composed by Bernard, the poem reflects the type of religious life he exemplified, combining a mystic faith and an emotional intensity that enabled him to lead kings, emperors, and popes.

Paul Gerhardt's translation of *Salve Caput cruentatum* was in turn paraphrased in English by former British poet laureate Robert Bridges (st.1–3 and 5) and American Presbyterian minister and scholar James Waddell Alexander (st.4). Thus, the hymn is the product of three different centuries, four different countries, and four different religious traditions, probably making it the most ecumenical of all hymns in popular use!

The tune with which the text is indelibly associated, PASSION CHORALE, was originally a German love song, "My Heart is Distracted by a Gentle Maid," first appearing in a 1601 collection of songs by Hans Leo Hassler. Hassler's tune is harmonized by Johann Sebastian Bach, who must have been especially fond of the Passion Chorale: it appears five times in his "St. Matthew Passion," twice in the "Christmas Oratorio," in five cantatas, and in a chorale prelude for organ. Brahms also used the melody in two chorale preludes for organ.

〜

On this Good Friday, think of all the depictions of the crucifixion you have seen throughout your life. Because Jesus' observant Jewish disciples took seriously the second commandment—"Thou shalt not make to thyself any graven image"—we have no drawings of the actual event. Artists across the centuries have had to imagine it. And in painting or sculpting their versions of that scene on Golgotha, they have created a visual theology. These images betrayed their beliefs about Jesus' death, and revealed a great deal about their own spiritual needs, as well.

I think of early icons of the crucifixion, in which Jesus is portrayed objectively as a timeless figure, a window through which the viewer can glimpse eternity. I think of the proud images of "Christus Rex," the King who conquered evil in the great struggle on the cross. I think of other crucifixes: the limp and beautiful body hanging on polished wood over a prie-dieu, or the strong carpenter carved by a contemporary sculptor, looking courageously toward the west end of a convent chapel I know.

But when I sing this hymn, I think of the crucifixion depicted on the Isenheim triptych. Painted by the early sixteenth-century German artist Grünewald for the hospital chapel of St. Anthony's monastery in Isenheim, the center-piece is the contorted body of the suffering Jesus. The fingers of his nail-pierced hands are splayed like great claws against a dark sky. The neck is absolutely limp, the sacred head, wounded with thorns, hangs heavily on his chest. The flesh is pock-marked, almost rotting.

On one side of the cross, Mary, rigid with horror, is held, fainting, in the arms of the beloved disciple John, and a grieving Magdalene reaches out in prayer. On the other side stands John the Baptist, carrying a prophetic book and gesturing towards his cousin.

There is no beauty in this crucifixion: "so marred was his appearance, beyond human semblance." (Isa.52:14) He has "no form or majesty that we should look at him, nothing in his appearance that we should desire him." (Isa.53:2) This crucifixion is shocking. It is the real human face of suffering and death, neither idealized nor prettified.

I remind myself that this crucifixion was painted for a

hospital chapel, where mortally ill people would be seeing it. Here was a lifeless Jesus to whom they could relate, when their own bodies were failing them. Here was a Jesus, who, by not masking the horrors of death, helped to banish its terror for the dying. This was a Jesus whose contorted body mirrored their own agonies of pain. Here was the Jesus they needed, their companion in the dreaded passage at life's end.

We all need to look at this Jesus once in a while, no matter what our preference in crucifixes, because this Jesus is the truth. This is the human Jesus, whose flesh was as mortal as ours. This is the human Jesus, who did not call legions of angels to his rescue, but went through it all, right up to the last death rattle. If we can be with him on this Good Friday, in this Isenheim crucifixion and in this Passiontide hymn, it will be easier to know that he is with us, when our day comes as well.

Holy Saturday

Hymn 172   Were you there when they crucified my Lord?
African-American spiritual

Although "slave songs" were long an integral part of the African-American culture, little was done to write them down until after the Civil War. In 1867, a collection called *Slave Songs of the United States* was published. In 1871, a blacksmith's son named George L. White formed a group of nine African-American singers in Nashville, Tennessee, and began a pilgrimage northward. Despite cold, hunger, ridicule, and difficulty in finding shelter, they persevered until

—in the words of W. E. B. Dubois—"a burst of applause in the Congregational Council at Oberlin revealed them to the world."[49]

Singing primarily before white congregations, they brought their music to the attention of enthusiastic audiences: "When the Fisk Jubilee Singers returned from Europe laden with unheard-of honours, the endorsement of the music critics of the Old World, and above all, with much money, America awakened to the fact that here, within her own borders, was an indigenous, unique, and unexploited art treasure."[50] After seven years of touring, they brought back a hundred and fifty thousand dollars to found Fisk University.

There soon was a demand for more publications of spirituals. But their audience was not the African-American community; the spirituals became, in large part, the property of college and university glee clubs and choruses. Composers like Antonin Dvořák eagerly adapted some of the melodies, notably in his "New World Symphony": "The so-called plantation songs are indeed the most striking and appealing melodies that have been found this side of the water. There is nothing in the whole range of composition that cannot be supplied with themes from this source."[51] It was not until the 1960s that spirituals finally returned to popularity in African-American communities through their use in the civil rights movement.

"Were you there when they crucified my Lord?" belongs to a type of African-American spiritual in which the melody is intended to be performed at a slow tempo, with sustained tones and long phrases. The first printed version of this spiritual appeared in William E. Barton's *Old Plantation Hymns*, published in Boston in 1899. Traditional performances of this spiritual would have had the structure of "call" and "response" which is typical of African music: each time the question of "Were you there?" is posed, the congregation repeats the question (the "response"). The phrases are short and repetitious, employing very few words, and performance practices often included body rhythm accompaniments, such as hand clapping, foot stomping, shouting, crying, swaying, and musical interjections.

"Were you there when they crucified my Lord?" was the first African-American spiritual to be printed in a major denominational hymnal when it appeared in *The Hymnal 1940*, the predecessor to *The Hymnal 1982*.

❧

"Oh!——Sometimes it causes me to tremble, tremble, tremble . . ."

I remember hearing once, in a lecture by a musicologist, that the entire African-American musical heritage—which produced not just spirituals like "Were you there?" but eventually flowered into a new musical style called jazz—began with a single sound: a moan.

It was the moan of people torn from their homeland; the moan of human cargo on a crowded ship sailing a vast sea which separated them from all that was familiar; the moan of people sold like chattel; the moan of men and women separated from spouses and children; the moan of beings considered less than human.

From that moaning the spirituals were born; they were, in Howard Thurman's words, "a source of rich testimony concerning life and death, because in many ways they are the voice, sometimes strident, sometimes muted and weary, of a people for whom the cup of suffering overflowed in haunting overtones of majesty, beauty, and power."[52]

"Oh!—Sometimes it causes me to tremble, tremble, tremble . . . ." It is appropriate that we reflect on the extended moan that is "Were you there?" as we keep vigil with the disciples and faithful women who did not know that Easter was about to dawn. This spiritual is much more than a simple Biblical narrative about something that happened in the past. It is an opportunity to grieve as if the events we sing about happened yesterday. Distances of time and space have been removed. We are invited to stand beside Jesus' disciples at the foot of the cross and to hear the thud of the hammer as he was nailed to the "tree" (with its subtle overtones of lynching). We are invited to see the warm blood flowing from his pierced side, and to help carry his cold body to the tomb.

We are also invited to join Jesus' friends in the paralysis of grief. It is a time when the memories of the day before are so overwhelming that the only possible response is to moan and to tremble. In the terrifying emptiness of the hours of this day, however, God is at work unseen, transforming death into life.

Easter Vigil

Hymn 176, 177 Over the chaos of the empty waters
Bonnell Spencer, OHC (1909–1996) A Monastic Breviary

A Monastic Breviary was compiled by the Order of the Holy Cross and the Order of Saint Helena and published in 1976. It contains the cycle of the "offices"—Matins, Diurnum, Vespers, and Compline—which are said daily by members of those religious orders. *A Monastic Breviary* includes much material that is ancient in origin, but it also includes the work of contemporary theologians. Bonnell Spencer, a monk of the Order of the Holy Cross, was editor of the volume, and wrote "Over the chaos of the empty waters" to be sung as a hymn for Vespers on Sundays.

Bonnell ("Bonnie") Spencer, born in 1909 in New York City, attended Trinity School, Williams College, Oxford University, and General Theological Seminary. In May of 1937, he was ordained a priest, and was life professed in the Order of the Holy Cross in 1940.

There followed a long and fruitful life, which included service as novice master, prior, assistant superior, member of the Standing Liturgical Commission as chair of its Christian Initiation Committee, and contributor to the revision of the Book of Common Prayer. He was a prolific writer and thoughtful teacher and valued greatly the time he spent in the Order's African mission. In a letter at the age of eighty-three, four years before his death, he wrote, "I keep well and busy. The high point of the past year was my visit to my beloved Ghana. I had a quiet and restful month at Philip Quaque Monastery, was present when the seminary I taught at began its fall term, and was even able to make a shelf check of the library I started back in 1983."[53]

In a letter to the editorial commission of *The Hymnal 1982*, Spencer pointed out "the parallel between 'the empty waters' and 'the empty tomb'," and the importance of the word "issued," with its overtones of birth, at the end of the first stanza. This baptismal or Easter hymn, particularly relevant when used at Baptism at the Great Vigil of Easter, has two fluid musical settings; the first one entitled WEST PARK, after the Mother House of the Order that Bonnell Spencer served so well.

❧

In high school, I learned about Isaac Newton, who believed that God's perfection was reflected above all in the world's natural orderliness. Newton's universe was predictable: the famous apple would always fall downwards. Chaos would not have been welcomed into his understanding of the world.

Chaos! Most of us are all too familiar with it! We struggle with emotional chaos, professional chaos, and social chaos. Most of us are still Newtonians at heart, and see chaos as negative, something to be put into order as soon as possible.

The contemporary science of quantum mechanics has introduced a different way of looking at the inevitable chaos of life. Scientists have discovered that Newton's insights do not apply at the subatomic level. The world of matter, for all its apparent solidity, is only congealed energy. Sub-atomic particles have a tendency to randomness, so specific events—unlike the apple's fall to the earth—cannot be predicted. In the eyes of contemporary physics, the world is still developing. Chaos is the arena of surprises, where the unexpected is likely to happen.

But is this insight actually so very new?

In the Mesopotamian and Canaanite myths of creation, Chaos was seen as the enemy—a monster with which the deity had to struggle. But the story told by our Hebrew ancestors was quite different. For them, chaos was no adversary; it was the cauldron of creation. God's spirit, hovering over the *tohu wobohu*—the "chaos of the empty waters"—brought forth the world from the chaos itself.

The story of God's power to bring forth a new creation from chaos is told and retold. From the chaotic waters of the flood came God's covenant with Noah. Into the chaos of the obedient Abraham's anguish came the voice of the angel,

"Do not lay your hand upon the lad," and the promise that his descendants would be as the stars of heaven and the sand on the seashore. Through the chaos of the Red Sea, the Israelites found freedom. Finally, in the early hours of Easter morning, from the dark chaos of death was born a new creation: the second Adam, the Risen Lord.

At every baptism, we reenact the bringing forth of new things from the cauldron of chaos. And we can begin to see that this is the pattern of our lives.

For the chaos in our lives is more like quantum mechanics than like Newtonian physics. Uncomfortable as it may be, it gives us the freedom to grow and to change, to continue to become, ourselves, "new creations."

Once I saw a display of "fractal images," computer-generated patterns that reproduce at ever smaller scales the irregular structures in nature as understood by quantum mechanics. They were images of astonishing beauty. They made me think of how boring an utterly predictable world would be. And they reminded me of the truth at the very core of our existence, the freedom God instilled in the smallest particles of our universe, and in our lives as well, and the new creations born from that freedom, as the Spirit hovers over us like a melody.

Easter Day

Hymn 203   Alleluia, alleluia! alleluia, alleluia!
  O sons and daughters, let us sing
Att. *Jean Tisserand (15th cent.)*; tr. *John Mason Neale (1818–1866)*

This hymn is possibly the work of the Franciscan Jean Tisserand, a popular preacher of his era, who was confessor to Anne of Brittany and founder of the Refuge de St. Madeleine, a community for the rehabilitation of prostitutes. He was a musician who composed a number of noëls in French and sequences in Latin. (On the other hand, it might have been written by *Jehan* Tisserand, a Dominican in the service of Louis de Bourbon, Bishop of Le Mans.)

No matter who wrote it, the hymn is an example of a narrative carol dating from the latter part of the Middle Ages. Originally entitled *L'alelya du jour des Pasques* ("Alleluia for Easter Day"), it is styled after a folk song with a refrain.

O filii et filiae is a paraphrase of Mt.28:1–7 and Jn.20:19:

> After the sabbath, as the first day of the week was dawning, Mary Magdalene and the other Mary went to see the tomb. And suddenly there was a great earthquake; for an angel of the Lord, descending from heaven, came and rolled back the stone and sat on it. His appearance was like lightning, and his clothing white as snow. For fear of him the guards shook and became like dead men. But the angel said to the women, "Do not be afraid; I know that you are

looking for Jesus who was crucified. He is not here; for he has been raised, as he said. Come, see the place where he lay. Then go quickly and tell his disciples, 'He has been raised from the dead,' and indeed he is going ahead of you to Galilee; there you will see him." (Mt.28:1–7)

When it was evening on that day, the first day of the week, and the doors of the house where the disciples had met were locked for fear of the Jews, Jesus came and stood among them and said, "Peace be with you." (Jn.20:19)

The music is a French carol melody, probably dating from the late fifteenth century.

ϾϿ

Given the popular nature of this hymn, I cannot resist picturing a group of townspeople enacting the drama—perhaps in front of the portico of their parish church, to celebrate this glorious festival.

I participated once in such an enactment, in a workshop designed to give people a deeper understanding of Scripture through movement. As we took each part, it was as if we took upon ourselves the emotions of each character. It was a powerful exercise. It is one thing to read about the faithful women who sought Jesus' tomb, and quite another to be one, walking slowly through the dawn, heavy with grief. I will never forget the sorrow—which had become a physical sensation—evaporating not just from our imaginations but from our bodies, as we heard the message of the angel. When we shifted to the personage of the angel, our bodies tingled with energy. Then we became the apostles, cowering in fear, until our Lord's presence brought us peace and courage.

During the "Alleluias," we were invited to improvise, letting the spirit of joy initiate our movement.

Movement is a powerful tool for understanding the truths of the Gospel, but perhaps this is most true on Easter. One of the ways to understand the story of Easter is as a metamorphosis from immobility to movement. This was true of the heavy-hearted women enclosed in their grief and of the trembling apostles imprisoned in their fear.

But above all, it was true of the One who on Good Friday was laid in a tomb sealed with a great stone. Like the moment in the dark movie theater when a projector breaks, movement was suspended. There was only stillness. No stretching and contracting of muscles. No pulsing of the heart. No breath.

But that stillness turned out to be the stillness of that split second between an exhalation and the next inhalation.

For on Easter, Jesus rose from the dead. "Christ is risen from the dead, trampling down death by death, and upon those in the tombs bestowing life," our Orthodox brothers and sisters sing. I like that idea of trampling; it conjures up the energy that changed the world in a split second.

It changed the world of the grieving women, and the trembling apostles. It helped them move again.

And it helps us move again, too, when we feel sealed in what we might describe as "tombs"—of grief, of fear, or helplessness. Jesus continues to trample down death by death, and to bestow life upon us in the tombs. Sometimes it means that our bodies will move again in freedom; but always it means that our spirits will move again.

Second Sunday of Easter

Hymn 212   Awake, arise, lift up your voice
Christopher Smart (1722–1771)

Walter Hussey, Dean of Chichester, once described the eighteenth-century poet Christopher Smart as "deeply religious, but of a strange and unbalanced mind."

Son of the steward of Lord Vane's estate in Kent, Smart attended Cambridge University's Pembroke Hall. He spent much of his time in taverns and got badly into debt. In spite of his irregularities he became fellow of Pembroke College, praelector in philosophy, and keeper of the common chest in 1745. For a period he was compelled to remain in his rooms for fear of creditors. A letter from that period by the poet Thomas Gray reports, "Smart must necessarily be abimé in a short time. His debts daily increase. . . . Our friend Lawman, the mad attorney, is his copyist; and truly the author himself is to the full as mad as he is."

After losing his Cambridge appointments in 1749, Smart moved to London and began writing poems and reviews under various pseudonyms. He married the stepdaughter of his publisher and became friends with Samuel Johnson, Burney, Garrick, and Hogarth. Boswell speaks in his *Life of Johnson* of "Christopher Smart, with whose unhappy vacillation of mind he [Johnson] sincerely sympathized." From 1750 to 1755, he annually won the Satonian Prize of Cambridge for a poem on a religious subject. In 1751, Smart began to show symptoms of mental aberration, which took the form of a compulsion to pray publicly, and he was confined to an asylum in 1756. Boswell records a visit Johnson made to him there:

> Concerning this unfortunate poet, Christopher Smart, who was confined in a mad-house, he had, at another time, the following conversation with Dr. Burney:
>
> BURNEY. "How does poor Smart do, Sir; is he likely to recover?"
>
> JOHNSON. "It seems as if his mind had ceased to struggle with the disease; for he grows fat upon it."
>
> BURNEY. "Perhaps, Sir, that may be from want of exercise."
>
> JOHNSON. "No, Sir; he has partly as much exercise as he used to have, for he digs in the garden. Indeed, before his confinement, he used for exercise to walk to the ale-house; but he was *carried* back again. I do not think he ought to be shut up. His infirmities were not noxious to society. He insisted on people praying with him; and I'd as lief pray with Kit Smart as any one else."[54]

Smart spent the years 1759–1763 in a private home for the insane in Bethnal Green. After leaving the asylum, he published his best known poem, *A Song of David*, but he soon declined into poverty and debt and spent his final days in a debtor's prison.

Many people know the poet through his work *Rejoice in the Lamb* in its musical setting by Benjamin Britten.

This hymn is one of the thirty-four *Hymns and Spiritual Songs for the Fasts and Festivals of the Church of England* appended to Christopher Smart's complete paraphrase of the psalter, *A Translation of the Psalms of David* (1765).

Scriptural echoes include 1 Eph.5:14 ("Sleeper, awake! Rise from the dead, and Christ will shine on you"); Phil.4:4 ("Rejoice in the Lord always; again I will say, Rejoice"), Mt.27:62–66 (Pilate's command that Jesus' tomb be sealed with a stone) and Jn. 20:19–29 (Jesus' appearance to the disciples and to "doubting" Thomas).

The music to this hymn dates, appropriately, from the same century as the text.

cs

The wounds remain. The hands and feet still bear the marks of the nails. But those wounds are the identifying mark of the crucified and risen Christ.

Jesus' risen body is not the body of a Greek statue without blemish; its blemishes are its badge.

We, who feel that we must meet standards of perfection in order to do God's work, can take heart. Perhaps, it is, above all, our wounds which enable us to heal and to love.

Physical wounds, which pierce our skin's protection, open our bodies to infection. We know we must not neglect them. They must be cleansed and protected from further irritation. And they must also be exposed to air. When they do heal, the skin is often scar-tissue, which is stronger than the skin it replaces.

There are other kinds of wounds we human beings bear: wounds to the spirit.

These wounds can become infected, as well. A moment of resentment can grow into hatred; a loss can become depression; a betrayal can become paranoia.

We need to care for these interior wounds through sound spiritual practices, just as we care for the wounds that pierce our bodies through sound medical practices. We must not neglect these wounds, or pretend they do not exist. We cleanse them by acknowledging them and letting ourselves feel the pain they bring us. We protect them by avoiding the additional irritation of dwelling on whatever wounded us. We expose them to the fresh oxygen breathed upon us by the Wounded Healer, Jesus himself.

I expect that Christopher Smart knew a great deal about the wounds of the spirit. With the wisdom of the so-called madman, "Kit" Smart knew the source of healing. When he felt imprisoned in his confusion, he recognized that Jesus as well had known friendlessness and rejection.

Christopher Smart's scars did not go away. Instead, they enabled that "strange and unbalanced mind" to write poetry that still speaks to us.

And our scars do not go away, either. They are the badges that tell us we have lived and suffered. And, with the help of the Wounded Healer, Jesus Christ, they can enable us to reach out to others, as we continue his work on earth.

Third Sunday of Easter

Hymn 296   We know that Christ is raised and dies no more

John Brownlow Geyer (b.1932)

John Brownlow Geyer was born in Yorkshire and studied at the Universities of Cambridge, Oxford, and Heidelberg. He is an ordained minister of the Congregational Union of Scotland, a union of Congregationalists and Presbyterians. A respected theologian and Biblical scholar, he has worked in parish ministry, and served as chaplain to the University of St. Andrew's Congregational students. He was also chaplain at conferences sponsored by the Royal School of

Church Music. His diaries, dating back to 1947 and still being written, will be lodged in the archives of Queen's College, Cambridge.

Concerning this hymn's inspiration, Geyer writes:

> "We know that Christ is raised" was written in 1967, when I was a tutor at Chestnut College, Cambridge, UK. At that time a good deal of work was going on round the corner (involving a number of American research students) producing living cells ('the baby in the test tube'). The hymn attempted to illustrate the Christian doctrine of baptism in relation to these experiments. Originally intended as a hymn for the Sacrament of Baptism, it has become popular as an Easter hymn.[55]

"We know that Christ is raised" is based on Rom. 6:9: "We know that Christ, being raised from the dead, will never die again; death no longer has dominion over him." The hymn is full of the baptismal imagery of water, death, and rebirth. There is a "new creation" on the occasion of a baptism, just as there was a "new creation" at Easter—the sacred equivalents of the miracles being wrought in the test tubes in the laboratories in Cambridge.

The strong tune ENGELBERG by the Irish-born composer Charles Villiers Stanford was the author's own choice for use with his text.

ↀ

Life is a miracle. When I am in danger of forgetting that, I think of friends who are in anguish because they long for children and are unable to conceive; and I understand the reason for the experiments being done in that Cambridge laboratory around the corner from John Geyer's Chestnut

College. And I remember with gratitude the moment of birth of each of our two sons, and marvel at the adults they have become, each one with his own genes bearing unique traits given him courtesy of my husband's and my family trees.

Even Life with a large "L" is a miracle. The Roman Catholic monk Sean Caulfield writes:

> God placed within the universe everything it needed for its development. But it was free and had to do its own developing, and that is where the chaos, the chance, and the unpredictable entered. . . . We should realize that life on this planet is sheer good fortune, an event that did not have to be. The chances of this hunk of matter developing life forms, the sheer improbability of the coming together of all the required circumstances which in harmony with one another had the power (from God's creative act) to bring about life here, must have been millions to one. That it developed here is marvelous good fortune for us. . . . One species of life, fortunately for us the "human," developed to where consciousness doubled back upon itself and became self-conscious. We began to reflect upon ourselves and be intelligent. This also was the result of God's creative act, so that ultimately it was he who "breathed into us the breath of life." The circumstances were happily correct; the lobes of the brain had developed. Yet, in this freedom world of ours, thousands of things could have gone wrong which might have prevented it. If the right mammoth lizard had eaten the right prehistoric humanoid at the right time, you might very well be eating this book right now instead of reading it.[56]

The Creator who imagined life for us at the beginning of creation must have been impelled by the love an artist holds for a creation to desire that our life not perish. And so there is another miracle. It is the miracle of the Resurrection, when Christ broke death's fearful embrace, and claimed that victory for us as well.

Our baptism reminds us of the cost of this gift of eternal life. We share his death by being "drowned" in the waters of baptism, rather than sealed in a tomb. We are clothed with the Spirit's power, as Jesus was clothed with the splendor of a risen body. We have become, in essence, new: our bodies are no longer our own, but part of Christ's body. We are sealed with the sign of the cross, which has become no longer a mark of death, but of the miracle of life.

Fourth Sunday of Easter

Hymn 243   When Stephen, full of power and grace
Jan Struther (1901–1953)

Jan Struther is best known as the author of *Mrs. Miniver*, the World War II novel about life in an English middle-class family. The novel, published in 1940, subsequently was made into a popular movie. She was educated privately and began publishing her writing at the age of sixteen, deriving her pen name from her maiden name, Joyce Anstruther. She was deeply involved in the preparation of the enlarged edition of *Songs of Praise* (1932), served on the editorial board of the London *Times*, and continued to write many articles, short stories, and poems. Besides *Mrs. Miniver*, she is also well known for her collection of essays and sketches entitled *Try Anything Twice* (1938) and her volume of serious poems, *The Glass-Blower* (1941). During the World War II years, she lived with her children in New York and was much in demand as a lecturer. She wrote of that sojourn, "My children are delighted when they hear taxi drivers say 'foist' and 'thoid' just as in films."[57] Cancer cut her life short in July of 1953.

The words of this hymn are a meditation on the life and ministry of Stephen, the church's first martyr, a story found in the sixth and seventh chapters of Acts. Luke tells of complaints that the widows of the Hellenists (or Greek-speaking Jews) were being neglected in the daily distribution of food by the disciples' community. The twelve agreed that they should not "neglect the word of God in order to wait on tables," and chose for the task of serving the poor "seven men of good standing, full of the Spirit and of wisdom." Stephen, "a man full of faith and the Holy Spirit," was among those chosen for this role. "Full of grace and power," Stephen did great wonders and signs, as well as preaching the Gospel. Most of the seventh chapter of Acts is his sermon before the high priest, which recounts the sacred history of God and the recalcitrant chosen people. It so enraged the listeners that they dragged him out of the city and stoned him. Following the pattern of Jesus, Stephen forgave his murderers and prayed, "Lord Jesus, receive my spirit."

The text is paired with a strong American folk melody.

☙

The story of Stephen reminds me that the church is often called to stand apart from the world. In every age, society needs a conscience, and one of the roles of the church and her people is to be that conscience.

Those who wield temporal power do not usually like to hear such messages. When Stephen reminded the high priest and his council that, as part of a "stiff-necked people," they had a long history of opposing the messages of the prophets and the work of the Holy Spirit, they became enraged. The same story has been repeated again and again throughout history. During the times in history when the church itself has become a temporal power, prophets like Stephen have inevitably arisen to remind it to return to its roots.

What does that mean for the church today, and for you and for me? I think that we need to be on our guard against becoming too comfortable. I often wonder if the quarrels within the church are a subtle method of avoiding the real issue: that the Gospel calls us to look outside ourselves, at the world around us, and to speak out when we see injustice being done.

But we can't wait for our institutions to do it. We must begin, ourselves, each one of us. For the church *is* ourselves.

The story of the first martyr Stephen can provide guidance for us.

> But only in his heart a flame
> and on his lips a sword
> wherewith he smote and overcame
> the foemen of the Lord.

We may think that one lone voice does not count, but we are likely to discover that, when our hearts are aflame and we speak the truth with love, people will pay attention to us. An e-mail to a member of Congress, a telephone call to a corporation, or a letter to the newspaper editor may seem like small things in a world where there is so much evil to be confronted. But, through us, they serve as God's sword.

But only in his heart a flame
and on his eyes a light
wherewith God's daybreak to proclaim
and rend the veils of night.

When we speak out, we are empowered not by anger and despair, but by love and hope. It is as if we have already felt the first rays of "God's daybreak."

But only in his heart a flame
and on his lips a prayer
that God, in sweet forgiveness' name,
should understand and spare.

Our spirits must be free of hatred. Although we confront evil, we must remember that the evildoer is a child of God, a human being with potential for change.

When we add our actions, however small they may seem to us, to the work of healing the world, we will not fret about the results. We will be able to leave the results in God's hands. And, although we may find ourselves standing outside the mainstream of society, we will discover it is the only place we want to be.

But only in my heart a flame
and in my soul a dream,
so that the stones of earthly shame
a jeweled crown may seem.

Fifth Sunday of Easter

Hymn 463, 464   He is the Way
W. H. Auden (1907–1973)

Wyston Hugh Auden, a major twentieth-century poet, was born in York, England, grew up in Birmingham, and was shipped off to boarding school where he began writing poetry. He entered Christ Church College, Oxford, where he formed firm friendships with Stephen Spender, Cecil Day Lewis and Christopher Isherwood; the group collaborated on poetry and were beneficiaries of the emancipating influence of T.S. Eliot. He lived in Berlin when Naziism was on the rise, and returned to England to work as a schoolmaster, although he continued to visit Germany regularly, staying with his friend and collaborator, Christopher Isherwood. His first volume of poems was accepted by T.S.Eliot at Faber and Faber. It was published in 1930, to great acclaim. In 1935, he met the composer Benjamin Britten, who was to set many of his poems to music.

Early in 1939, Auden left with Isherwood for the United States, where he met Chester Kallman, who became his life-long friend and companion. In the early 1940s, following the death of Auden's devout Anglo-Catholic mother, his poetry became increasingly Christian in tone. He returned to England in 1956 to become Professor of Poetry, and then a Fellow, at Oxford, where he spent much of his time during the last years of his life. He died suddenly in Vienna.

Auden's obituary from the *New York Times* of September 30, 1973, states:

The singular voice of W. H. Auden gave resonance to a troubled age. . . . His sermons to modern man were artfully concealed within the forms of rhyme. . . . "In a world of prayer," he wrote, "we are all equal in the sense that each of us is a unique person, with a unique perspective on the world, a member of a class of one." . . . [T]he voice that issued from his seared and craggy face was like no other on earth. It could sing lyrically and it could speak plain. Auden delivered his lines from a perspective unmatched, a member of a class of one.

"He is the Way" is the final chorus of Auden's poem *For the Time Being: A Christmas Oratorio*, written between 1941 and 1942 and dedicated to his mother: "In memoriam Constance Rosalie Auden, 1870–1941." It was intended as a libretto for an extended work by Benjamin Britten, which the composer never completed. A setting was composed, however, by Marvin David Levy (b.1932). Its first performance, in 1959, was conducted in New York by Margaret Hillis.

Each stanza begins with an allusion to Jn. 14:6 ("Jesus said to him, 'I am the way, and the truth, and the life.'"), followed by surreal poetic language that challenges our imaginations.

Both contemporary musical settings—by David Hurd and Richard Wetzel—invite us into the exotic landscape suggested by the poetry.

☙

What do these strange words mean?

Perhaps that is not the question we ought to ask. Instead, we might ask, "How do these words make me feel?"

I think that it was C. S. Lewis who said that good

religious literature does not tell about belief; instead, it gives the reader the feeling of what it is to believe.

This is where the art of poetry excels. Poetry like Auden's compels us to understand, not with our intellect alone, but with our heart and imagination. It does not preach at us. Rather, it initiates a conversation between the author's words and the reader's thought.

Good religious poetry, indeed, may be faith's most accurate literature, because it refuses to spell things out. Instead, like a Russian icon, it serves as a window through which we glimpse the divine. Poetry's images and paradoxes can jar us into seeing the invisible behind the visible world.

Good religious poetry is like good liturgy; a partnership of the mind and the body, the heart and the imagination, the seen and the unseen. Its language is not abstraction, but image and metaphor. It beckons us to think in a more holistic way, leaving behind for a while our demand for linear logic.

We can best approach a poem like Auden's as we do a parable, letting it live and breathe in us, and forgetting, for a while, our need for answers.

Another twentieth-century poet once wrote to a young high school student, whose research paper on his work he had carefully read: "Like all other critics, you attribute to me conscious intentions here and there of which I was certainly not aware. But you must remember that there is a difference always between what the author meant and what the poem means to the reader. With best wishes, Yours sincerely, T. S. Eliot."[58]

We "understand" poetry not by trying to figure logically what the poet intended, as I had done at the age of seventeen, but by letting poetry's images reverberate in both our conscious and our unconscious minds.

Auden's text entices me into the unique and startling terrain through which the Way of Christ may take me. It expands my vision so that I can see the Truth: that my anxiety and God's reassurance are eternally intertwined. It dances in me, inviting me to lift my gaze to the Life around me—my husband and children and other neighbors on this earth—and to find Christ there.

Auden's images may say something entirely different to you, but, then, his publisher, T. S. Eliot, would say that is exactly the way it should be.

Sixth Sunday of Easter

Hymn 394, 395   Creating God, your fingers trace
Jeffery Rowthorn (b.1934)

Jeffery A. Rowthorn, a native of Wales, is a graduate of Cambridge and Oxford Universities, Union Theological Seminary in New York City, and Cuddesdon Theological College, Oxford. He served in the Royal Navy and was ordained a deacon in 1962 and priest in 1963 in the Church of England. He served as curate at Woolwich Parish Church in Southeast London, and as rector of St. Mary's Church, Garsington, Oxford, before being appointed dean of instruction and chaplain at Union Theological Seminary. He went to Yale University in 1973 as a founding faculty member of the Institute of Sacred Music, where he served as chapel minister at Berkeley Divinity School and became the first holder of Berkeley's Bishop Percy Goddard Chair in Pastoral Theology. In 1987, he was consecrated Bishop

Suffragan of Connecticut. Upon his resignation in 1993 from that position, Bishop Rowthorn was appointed Bishop of the American Convocation of Churches in Europe with his residence in Paris.

Rowthorn has edited two hymnals, published a two-volume collection of litanies, and written many hymn texts.

When he was teaching at Yale Divinity School, Rowthorn assigned his class the task of paraphrasing a psalm. Deciding to write his own as well, he recast the fourteen-verse Psalm 148 into a hymn of four stanzas, each opening with an address to God—"creating," "sustaining," "redeeming," and "indwelling." In the tradition of Isaac Watts, he made the psalm universal, substituting for the phrase "children of Israel" his own line, "one family with a billion names," and expanding the original text to include among God's creatures those who are "despised for creed or race."

Without Rowthorn's knowledge, the text was submitted to the 1979 Hymn Society of America's "New Psalms for Today" competition, and was selected as the winner of one of the two prizes.

This hymn can be sung to a setting written early in this century by an English composer, or to a melody by the contemporary American David Hurd.

∽

I like to think of God as an artist. God's artistry is obvious to me when I step outside on a starry night, or glimpse the soft moon on a misty evening, or gasp at a sunset. I love this wondrous earth, God's creation.

The more I learn about this planet, the more I am in awe of God's artistry. What I have discovered is that the more I learn, the more I discover there is yet to learn; for the earth is infinitely complex. I think of the lines about the atmosphere—"water's fragile blend with air, enabling life"—from Lewis Thomas's 1974 classic, *Lives of a Cell*:

> Taken all in all, the sky is a miraculous achievement. It works, and for what it is designed to accomplish it is as infallible as anything in nature. I doubt whether any of us could think of a way to improve on it, beyond maybe shifting a local cloud from here to there on occasion. The word 'chance' does not serve to account well for structures of such magnificence.[59]

There is a delightful children's book by Crockett Johnson, *Harold and the Purple Crayon*, in which a little boy draws a world full of adventures with a crayon. When he becomes immersed in some wavy lines he has drawn, he quickly draws a boat. When he gets hungry, he draws a picnic blanket covered with rows of pies. When he gets full, he draws an animal to finish off the pies. Finally, he searches in vain for his home, the place from which he had set out. He draws houses and more houses, until he remembers what the moon looked like seen through the window beside his bed. He draws the window, and the moon, and there he is: in his own room again.

The world Harold draws is a dynamic world. Everything he draws has an effect on what he drew before; in response to his most recent drawing, he always needs to draw something else.

Our universe is like Harold's purple crayon world, rather than like a finished painting hung in an art museum or living room. Its pattern is one of movement—dynamic, not static. Scientists doing research on weather patterns, for example, make the startling assertion that the flutter of a butterfly's wings in Tokyo will eventually have an effect on the weather in Texas.

It is not surprising that our artist God who has created such an amazing design should continue to sustain it, "uphold[ing] earth's mysteries known or yet untold." When the design goes awry—when some creatures are excluded from the beauty their creator intended—any artist would wish to put things right, embracing with compassion those who have been neglected or despised. And the artist's spirit surely dwells within every work of art.

Our glimpses here on earth of the work of our creating, sustaining, redeeming, indwelling God help to prepare us for eternal beauty. When we understand this, we, who are also the work of the Artist's hands, cannot help but join in a chorus of thanksgiving and praise.

Ascension Day

Hymn 215   See the Conqueror mounts in triumph
Christopher Wordsworth (1807–1885)

The son of a scholarly clergyman and nephew of the celebrated poet William Wordsworth, Christopher Wordsworth was renowned in his own right. Born in Lambeth while his father was rector there, Wordsworth went to Cambridge, where he had a brilliant career in both classics and mathematics. He eventually became a Fellow, classical lecturer, and public orator at the university. He had close contact with his noted uncle through regular correspondence and frequent visits with him at Rydal in the Lake District until the poet's death in 1850. Wordsworth was successively headmaster of the fine preparatory school Harrow, canon of Westminster Abbey, vicar of Stanford-in-the-Vale-cum-Goosey in Berkshire, archdeacon of Westminster, and finally Bishop of Lincoln.

His nineteen years in Berkshire brought out the teacher and pastor in him. He tailored his hymns to his parishioners, using hymns in simple and direct language to teach about the church's festivals, beliefs, and heritage. Wordsworth preferred objective and didactic hymns to subjective ones. He wrote that hymns are "one of the most efficacious instruments for correcting error and disseminating truth, as well as for ministering comfort and edification . . . .it is the first duty of a hymn to teach sound doctrine."[60]

A contemporary of his wrote, "He was a most holy, humble, loving, self-denying man. And the man is reflected in his verse. To read one of his best hymns is like looking into a plain face, without one striking feature, but with an irresistible charm of honesty, intelligence, and affection."[61]

The stately music is an appropriate match for a text in which the Ascension of Jesus is seen as the glorious entry into heaven of a triumphant king.

ᏩᎦ

In Brian Swimme's book *The Universe is a Green Dragon*, there is a chapter on "Allurement," which contains an imaginary dialogue between a youth and the Roman Catholic priest Thomas Berry. Berry speaks of "allurement," or attraction, as the universal force that permeates the entire universe. One of its forms is gravity, which keeps the galaxies from breaking apart, and keeps you and me from spinning off into space.[62]

When I see Renaissance paintings of the Ascension, I

see a Jesus who defies gravity, who literally goes "up" to heaven. If you or I were to go "up," where would we go? To a "heaven" light-years beyond the galaxies? To another dimension of reality, one which we do not experience in our ordinary lives on earth? As one of my seminary professors answered such questions, it is a "great mystery."

But the fact remains that Luke's second book, the Acts of the Apostles, tells us that Jesus was lifted up into the clouds, out of the sight of the astonished apostles.

We question, "How could this be?" And we ask, further, "What does it have to do with us?"

Perhaps the key to the answer lies in that idea of "allurement." The Ascension may be seen as the demonstration of another kind of gravity, different from the force that helps us keep our feet on the ground. It is the force of our destiny with God. Through our risen and ascended Lord, we are pulled towards that destiny, as fragments of iron to a magnet.

In Christopher Wordsworth's triumphal hymn, the Ascension of Jesus is depicted as the return of a victorious king to his palace. But we are part of that story also. "Thou hast raised our human nature on the clouds to God's right hand. . . . Man with God is on the throne."

We are meant ultimately for union with God. Paul writes that "all of us, with unveiled faces, seeing the glory of the Lord as though reflected in a mirror, are being transformed into the same image from one degree of glory to another; for this comes from the Lord, the Spirit." (2 Cor.3:18) "The glory that you have given me I have given them," writes John the Evangelist. (Jn.17:22)

That is a difficult truth for the human mind to grasp. Perhaps the Ascension was God's way of teaching us that "in thine ascension, we by faith behold our own."

Seventh Sunday of Easter

Hymn 460, 461   Alleluia! sing to Jesus!
William Chatterton Dix (1837–1898)

William Chatterton Dix was the son of a well-known Bristol surgeon and author. He was educated at the Bristol Grammar School, and later became manager of a marine insurance company in Glasgow. A scholarly layman who combined a successful business career with a gift for hymn writing, Dix published several volumes of hymns and devotional works, and rendered a number of Greek and Abyssinian hymns and sequences into metrical form.

"Alleluia! sing to Jesus!," entitled by Dix "Redemption by the Precious Blood," first appeared in Dix's collection *Altar Songs, Verses on the Holy Eucharist* (London, 1867).

Scriptural allusions include Jn.6:32 ("I am the bread of life"); Ps.78:25 ("So mortals ate the bread of angels"); Rev.4:6 ("and in front of the throne there is something like a sea of glass, like crystal"); and Rev.5:9 ("They sing a new song: 'You are worthy to take the scroll and to open its seals, for you were slaughtered and by your blood you ransomed for God saints from every tribe and language and people and nation'").

The hymn conflates the image of monarch ("his the scepter, his the throne") and high priest ("thou within the veil hast entered, robed in flesh, our great High Priest"). The latter image is based on Heb.9:11–14:

> But when Christ came as a high priest of the good
> things that have come, then through the greater and

perfect tent (not made with hands, that is, not of this creation), he entered once for all into the Holy Place, not with the blood of goats and calves, but with his own blood, thus obtaining eternal redemption. For if the blood of goats and bulls, with the sprinkling of the ashes of a heifer, sanctifies those who have been defiled so that their flesh is purified, how much more will the blood of Christ, who through the eternal Spirit offered himself without blemish to God, purify our conscience from dead works to worship the living God!

The writer of Hebrews refers to the Jewish cultic observation of the Day of Atonement. Earlier in Chapter 9, he refers to a "tent": the portable shrine used in the days before the building of Solomon's temple. This tent had an outer court, the Holy Place, and an inner court, the Holy of Holies, which held the ark of the covenant. On one day of the year, Yom Kippur, the Day of Atonement, the high priest passed through the curtain which normally barred access to the divine presence, to offer the blood of the sacrifices as a propitiation for his own sins and those of his people.

This jubilant hymn is set to the popular Welsh hymn tune HYFRYDOL, which, appropriately, means "joyful," and also to the tune by Samuel Sebastian Wesley written especially for the text.

ॐ

The priestly imagery in "Alleluia! sing to Jesus!" may be inspired by the Epistle to the Hebrews, but the royal atmosphere is straight out of Dix's Victorian England. Although the monarch's imperial power is a thing of the past, England still cherishes its royal traditions. If you have ever seen the movie of Queen Elizabeth II's coronation, with its pomp and pageantry, you have some idea of what I mean.

Sometimes the church's worship reflects this kind of splendor. I have had occasion to sing this hymn in procession in stately liturgies replete with all the paraphernalia that Anglicans love: music, torches, processional crosses, incense, beautiful vestments. I love walking in processions like this. Although I am basically an introvert, I have enough of the extrovert in me that I love to move down the aisle singing "Alleluia!" to a rousing tune.

But the scholarly and thoughtful Dix sneaks an ambiguous note into the triumphant procession. We sweep down the aisle until we are caught up short by the word at the end of the first stanza: blood. Blood! We continue, however, singing that earth is Jesus' footstool and heaven his throne, until our throat catches again, at the phrase "thou on earth both Priest and Victim." This scepter was gained at a cost.

Contemporary Christians sometimes criticize the use of royal and high priestly imagery for Jesus. Over history, such triumphal symbols may well have contributed their share to the excesses of the church. The church's worldly power may have seemed at one time a thoroughly appropriate reflection of its Lord's royalty. Its ecclesiastical power may have been considered a proper use of its Lord's authority as great High Priest. But because people within the church as well as outside it are all too human, this power has often led to corruption. Those who reject this triumphal imagery prefer to focus, instead, on the cost of Jesus' victory. They emphasize Jesus' servanthood and solidarity with the common people.

Dix's hymn reminds me that one of the glories of the Christian tradition is that we can have it both ways. We can march in glorious processions, and then trade our vestments for aprons in order to feed the victims of hunger in a soup kitchen. We can sing Jesus' praises in churches glowing with the reds, blues, and greens of glorious stained glass, and then stand in silent vigil on the village square for the end of bloodshed around the world. Both are the truth. In both, we celebrate our Lord, who reigns both in the heavenly courts and in the hearts of his most humble brothers and sisters on earth. Alleluia!

The Day of Pentecost

Hymn 506, 507   Praise the Spirit in creation
Michael Hewlett (b. 1916)

An English parish priest in charge of four hamlets in Devon, Michael Hewlett has written close to 100 hymns. He writes, "I regard hymn writing as a branch of religious journalism, requiring some of the same gifts, and would recommend others not to aspire to be poets, but to take their inspiration from technicians like W. S. Gilbert, Irving Berlin, and Oscar Hammerstein II."[63] His hymns were, like those of the aforementioned composers, aimed at an audience: his parishioners. They were written because he needed a particular kind of hymn for a particular day. Hewitt wrote this hymn to satisfy a need for a processional hymn on Whitsunday, and entitled it "A Whitsun Procession."

This hymn, containing the dynamic images described in Acts 2:1–11, fills a need for hymnody for Pentecost and the Holy Spirit and encompasses the whole range of the Spirit's work.

The first stanza refers to the Spirit in creation, moving over the face of the waters (Gen.1:2) and giving life-breath to the first creature (Gen.2:7). In the second, Hewlett writes of the Spirit within, in our thoughts, our wonder, and our conscience. He next speaks of the Spirit's inspiration in the prophets and priests of our tradition, in the Spirit of Jesus, and in the "truth behind the wisdoms which as yet know not our Lord"—other world religions and philosophies. The fourth stanza describes the Pentecost event as a time when Jesus "armed a people for his own," so that they would carry his message to the furthest corners of the known world, turning it "upside down." The fifth stanza is a prayer, asking the flame of the Spirit to descend on us, so that we also would, "white-hot in your possession . . . set the world alight." The final doxology emphasizes the "oneness" of the Trinity ("in deep accord"). It concludes with the paradox that when we sing the praises of the "Source, Truth, and Inspiration," we are doing so through the inspiration of that same Trinity.

The text is paired with two tunes: the first one a strong procession and the second written in very lyric style.

ᚙ

Ruach. When I say that Hebrew word, ending with an explosive rush of breath, I am naming God's Spirit in the language of the Book of Genesis. The sound of the word itself suggests the restless Spirit moving over the face of the waters in Gen. 1:2. It suggests the infusion of life to the clay figure modeled by God's hand in Gen. 2:7.

The creation stories in Genesis, which so gracefully convey theological truth through dramatic narrative, help to illuminate the story of Pentecost, as well as the work of the Spirit today in our lives.

Ruach was the energy of creation; it was the breath of life.

I am reminded of the equation: *adamah* ("dust from the earth") plus *ruach* equals *adam* ("human being"). I am reminded that God's life-giving Spirit is as integral to human identity as our bodies. It is a gift, animating all of us: our bodies, our hearts, our brains, even those unseen parts that we call the imagination, the psyche, the human spirit, or the soul.

To understand what happened with God's *ruach* on Pentecost, I think about what happens when I venture forth on cross-country skis on a cold snowy day. Because cross-country skiing is highly aerobic, by the time I return to our home, I feel as if my lungs have expanded to at least twice their capacity. And I also feel as if there is an oven inside my body. Even with the wind chill factor hovering near zero, I am not cold—with the occasional exception of my fingertips and toes. When I step inside our warm house, I feel as if I am on fire. My breath has produced heat, in an elemental alchemy. Air has generated fire.

On the day of Pentecost, *ruach*, like the rush of a mighty wind, filled the disciples, setting them ablaze with a life-force that was the gift of God. It was, in part, a re-enactment of Gen.2:7: God took humans, creatures of earth, and breathed the new life of Christ into them. "Air" had generated fire.

The work of the Spirit continues to bring both air and fire to the world. We recognize the presence of God's *ruach* when we find our hearts (in the words of John Wesley) "strangely warmed" by the presence of God as we pray. We feel it when some unseen "breeze" blows the cobwebs away from our brain and we see with clarity an issue with which we have been struggling. We hear it in the inspirations (or in-breathings of *ruach*) of thinkers and artists from every land and from every generation.

The life-breath of *ruach* is a gift. But, like the skier who ventures forth to exercise on a cold morning, we can increase our breathing capacity.

A very ancient way of prayer is the "breath-prayer," in which the person praying focuses on the very action of inhalation and exhalation while focusing on God.

"Praise the Spirit in creation" can become a breath-prayer. Whether we have a tape of the music, or just hear the text in our imaginations, Michael Hewlett's hymn can help us focus on God as we sit quietly and breathe to the rhythm of the words.

This is a different kind of "aerobic exercise," opening our spirits to the *ruach* that wants to break out within us like wind and like flame.

Trinity Sunday

Hymn 370   I bind unto myself today
Att. *Patrick (372–466)*; tr. *Cecil Frances Alexander (1818–1895)*

Of great antiquity, "I bind unto myself today" has been attributed to St. Patrick since at least the year 690.

St. Patrick was born in Britain to a noble family who had been Christians for at least three generations. When he was sixteen, he was captured by raiders from Ireland, who carried him away to be sold as a slave. He spent the following six years feeding livestock. Patrick eventually escaped, and probably went to study at Lérins, an abbey on a Mediterranean island off the coast of Cannes, between 412–415, at the end of which time he was ordained. In 431, he returned to Ireland as a missionary, and was consecrated Bishop of Ireland the following year. Patrick spent the rest of his life in converting the Irish people to Christianity, which involved not only organizing churches but also contending with the leaders of the native Druidic cult.

"I bind unto myself today" is an example of a Lorica, or "breastplate prayer," to be chanted while dressing oneself or arming for battle.

In the eleventh century manuscripts, the hymn is prefaced by the following story of its origin:

> Patrick made this hymn; in the time of Loegaire mac Neill [the Druidic chief] it was made, and the cause of its composition was for the protection of himself and his monks against the deadly enemies that lay in ambush for the clerics. And it is a lorica of faith for the protection of body and soul against demons and men and vices: when any person shall recite it daily with pious meditation on God, demons shall not dare to face him, it shall be a protection to him against all poison and envy, it shall be a guard to him against sudden death, it shall be a lorica for his soul after his decease.
>
> Patrick sang it when the ambuscades were laid for him by Loegaire, in order that he should not go to Tara to sow the Faith, so that on that occasion they were seen before those who were lying in ambush as if they were wild deer having behind them a fawn . . . and "Deer's Cry" is its name.[64]

The Scriptural references include Eph.6:13–14 ("Therefore take up the whole armor of God, so that you may be able to withstand on that evil day, and having done everything, to stand firm. Stand therefore, and fasten the belt of truth around your waist, and put on the breastplate of righteousness.") and 1 Thess.5:8 ("But since we belong to the day, let us be sober, and put on the breastplate of faith and love, and for a helmet the hope of salvation.")

Cecil Frances Alexander wrote the metrical version of Patrick's hymn for the 1891 revision of the *Irish Church Hymnal.* It is paired with two Irish melodies, the stirring St. Patrick's Breastplate and the contrasting Dierdre.

∽

There are two kinds of protective armor. One kind is represented by the Great Wall of China, built to protect China from her enemies, or the shining armor worn by medieval knights in battles or tournaments. The contemporary versions of that kind of armor are the bombs, guns, and all the pernicious paraphernalia of destruction stockpiled by the nations of the world, and even by some individuals. This kind of armor is meant to protect our bodies from destruction, or at least discourage those who would hurt us.

But does such armor protect the soul?

I know it doesn't work for me. Even when our outward physical safety is assured, most of us sometimes feel vulnerable and afraid. We may feel overwhelmed by the barrage of violent and fearful images we see on the evening news or read in the newspaper. We may feel paralyzed by tragedies in our neighborhood or bad news in our family. It is as if an "enemy" has breached our inner defenses, and we become captive to helplessness.

That is when we realize we need the other kind of armor: the power of the "Lorica": we can bind unto ourselves the strong Name of the Trinity.

There is great power in the images we allow to occupy our minds. When I was a child, I was taken to see the movie *Mrs. Miniver*, and I was terrified by a scene in which a wounded German airman enters Mrs. Miniver's home and holds her at gunpoint. That scene was so memorable that, when I recently saw the movie again, I was in my imagination the frightened little girl who was so sure that the faraway war my parents talked about in hushed voices would one day bring similar soldiers into our kitchen. And then I remembered, equally vividly, a dream I had shortly after seeing the movie over fifty years ago: that the Germans had invaded, and that I had started to say the Lord's Prayer and felt safe and protected.

That is the point of the Lorica. It is not only a prayer for God's protection: it also armors us spiritually with the images of God. The little girl who prayed the "Our Father" in her dream—perhaps drawing on an instinct bequeathed by her Celtic forebears—was able to defend her psyche against fear, even while she slept.

St. Patrick's Lorica of the Holy Trinity teaches us some of the ways to invite God's power to defend our souls: through meditation on the Gospel story, through the companionship of our ancestors in the faith, through our connection with creation, and through dependence on God's fidelity.

But I like to think of a Lorica as any way that helps us weave our awareness of God's presence around our lives "like the Celtic patterns on stones and in the illuminated Gospels."[65] Whether we defend ourselves with St. Patrick's hymn—or the Lord's prayer, a beloved Psalm, a session of Christian yoga or tai chi, a reassuring mantra, or silent contemplation—we have chosen the only armor adequate for the soul's protection. When our souls are afraid, earthly armor will not do; it is prayer alone that can clothe us with the eternal power of the Trinity.

Proper 1: *The Sunday closest to May 11*

Same as on the Sixth Sunday after Epiphany
(see page 56)

Proper 2: *The Sunday closest to May 18*

Same as on the Seventh Sunday after Epiphany
(see page 59)

Proper 3: *The Sunday closest to May 25*

Same as on the Eighth Sunday after Epiphany
(see page 62)

Proper 4: *The Sunday closest to June 1*

Hymn 636, 637   How firm a foundation, ye saints of the Lord
K. in John Rippon's *Selection (1787)*

The words of this text originally carried the title "Exceeding great and precious Promises." (2 Pet.3:4) It made its first appearance in 1787 in the second edition of *A Selection of*

Hymns from the Best Authors, Intended as an Appendix to Dr. Watt's Psalms and Hymns edited by John Rippon. The author of "How firm a foundation," who signed himself "K," may have been Richard Keen, the music director of the Baptist congregation in London where Rippon was minister. The hymnal became popular immediately in England. The American edition, printed by the Philadelphia Baptist Churches in 1820, met with similar acclaim, and it became known as the unofficial hymn textbook for the Baptists.

Andrew Jackson asked that the "How firm a foundation" be sung at his bedside as he was dying, and the hymn became well-known throughout both the North and South during the Civil War. Robert E. Lee requested it for his funeral hymn "as an expression of his full trust in the ways of the Heavenly Father." It was one of Theodore Roosevelt's favorite hymns and sung at his funeral.

The hymn could be considered a sermon in verse, using the following texts:

1. 2 Pet.3:4. In answer to the query, "Where is the promise of his coming?" comes the answer, "What more can God do than to send Jesus, God's word?"

2 Tim.2:19. "But God's firm foundation stands, bearing this inscription: "The Lord knows those who are his. . . ."

2. Isa.41:10. ". . . do not fear, for I am with you, do not be afraid, for I am your God; I will strengthen you, I will help you, I will uphold you with my victorious right hand."

3. Isa.43:2. "When you pass through the waters, I will be with you; and through the rivers, they shall not overwhelm you. . . ."

4. 2 Cor.12:9. "My grace is sufficient for you, for power is made perfect in weakness."

5. Heb.13:5. ". . . for he has said, 'I will never leave you or forsake you.'"

Both hymn tunes provided—the vigorous melody from *The Sacred Harp* and the strong eighteenth-century tune—underscore the strength of the text.

☙

This hymn can serve as a perfect example of "kinetic theology": letting the movement of our own bodies teach us about God. I would suggest that, for this meditation, you rise from your chair. Thinking "on your feet" will demonstrate a way that your physical response to a text can become a prayer.

"How firm a foundation." Take off your shoes and stand on the floor, preferably a hard surface rather than a carpet. Have you ever taken the foundation of the earth beneath you for granted? (If you have ever lived in a region prone to earthquakes, you would know that you cannot!)

Notice the contact of each part of the soles of your feet with the floor. Stand tall, and notice the weight of your body pulled by gravity toward the earth. Just as your body is pulled towards the foundation under you by that universal force, you stand on another, even firmer foundation: the foundation of God's promises through Jesus Christ.

But you need not merely stand. Shift your weight from foot to foot, as if you were walking in place. Then begin to walk, very deliberately, paying attention to the shift of your weight from foot to foot as you move. Still the floor does not move; rather, it supports your walk.

In similar fashion, God's "foundation" supports you as

you move through life. Begin to walk in the rhythm of the hymn, stepping forward on the strong accents of the text. Feel the energy and strength of your movement.

Continue walking in this way as you continue through the hymn. You may have to hold the text in your hand, unless you have it memorized or have a recording. Put yourself into the text imaginatively, as you read (or hear) each stanza. How might your body feel, when fear and dismay enter at the beginning of the second stanza? Would your steps become more hesitant, and your stance less erect, until you heard God's assurance? ("Fear not, I am with thee; O be not dismayed!") How would it feel to walk through deep waters, or through fiery trials? How would it feel if "all hell" should endeavor to shake your progress?

In the Buddhist tradition, there is a slow meditative prayer practice known as a "meditation walk." You might consider the exercise I have just described an alternative version of a Buddhist meditation walk, one that would be suitable for active Christian leaders like Jackson, Lee or Teddy Roosevelt, who must face many obstacles.

But all of us need to be reminded that, in our pilgrimage through life, we are sustained and upheld by the foundation of God's promises in Christ Jesus—and that we will never, no never, no never be forsaken by our Lord.

Proper 5: *The Sunday closest to June 8*

Hymn 701   **Jesus, all my gladness**
Johann Franck (1618–1677); tr. *Arthur Wellesley Wother-spoon (1853–1936)*

Johann Franck was born in Guben, Germany, the son of a lawyer. His father died when he was only two, and Franck's uncle, the town judge, adopted him and provided him with an excellent education. His uncle eventually sent him to study law at the University of Königsberg, the only German university left undisturbed by the Thirty Years War. Student life there was apparently extremely lively, but it did not distract the young Franck: "his religious spirit, his love of nature, and his friendship with such men as Simon Dach and Heinrich Held [also a hymnwriter], preserved him from sharing in the excesses of his fellow-students."[66]

He returned home two years later at the urgent request of his mother, who, fearful because of the presence in Guben of both Swedish and Saxon troops, wished to have him nearby. Soon he began practice as a lawyer; he became burgess and councillor, then burgomaster. Eventually he was appointed deputy to the Landtag (Diet) of Lower Lusatia.

Despite his successful career, however, Franck's fame today rests on his gifts as a poet rather than on his abilities as a lawyer. In 1877, to mark the bicentenary of his death, a monumental plaque honoring his memory was placed on the outer wall of Guben's Stadtkirche.

During his lifetime, one hundred of Franck's hymns were published. They reflect a transition in German hymnody:

from the objective church song of earlier Reformation hymnody to hymns of a more subjective nature. The hymnologist Julian writes, "In [Franck's] hymns we miss the objectivity and congregational character of the older German hymns, and notice a more personal, individual tone; especially the longing for the inward and mystical union of Christ with the soul as in his *Jesu, meine Freude*."[67]

Jesu, meine Freude ("Jesus, all my gladness") was modeled on *flora, meine Freude*, a love song written by Heinrich Alberti in 1641. The translation in *The Hymnal 1982* is that of the Scottish cleric, Arthur Wellesley Wotherspoon, for the *Scottish Mission Hymnbook* (1912).

The text was matched with its tune in 1656, when Johann Crüger set it to music. Johann Sebastian Bach later based a great five-part motet on the text and tune, and also used the tune in four of his cantatas and in several organ works.

❧

Christian spirituality is remarkable for its diversity. People understand God in different ways; they relate to God in different ways; they pray in different ways. That is true even within specific traditions; and anyone who is involved in the life of the church knows that it is true even within parishes.

One of the ways we can gain perspective on that diversity, and at the same time gain self-understanding about our own search for God, is to ask the question: "Which person of the Trinity is the most important in my life?"

Is it the first person of the Trinity, the Creator? Do you experience God as the "great I AM," the "Most High," the unnameable mystery who dwells at the heart of all things? Do you experience God through the creation—through the wondrous world of nature? Are you most comfortable with the wordless prayer of contemplation, leaving behind images and thoughts and letting yourself just "be" in relation to the mystery of God?

Or is it the Holy Spirit? Do you experience God as dynamic energy moving through your life, urging you to prayer and to action? Do you gain understanding of God through coincidences, through inspiration and intuition, and through your zeal to convey the Gospel to other people? Does that same kind of dynamic energy infuse your prayer? On the one hand, you may thrive on the excitement of great gatherings of God's people for worship; on the other hand, you may have a keen awareness of God's guidance in your personal prayer.

Or is it Jesus who is all your gladness? Do you long for Jesus as a beloved friend, who will be your repose, your joy, and your constant companion? When you read about him in the Gospel, does your heart leap? Is he an almost tangible, personal presence in your life? When you pray, do you picture his face?

The wonderful thing about all of these questions is that there are no right or wrong answers. The Creator, the Spirit, and the Son are "in one accord." When you relate to one of them, you relate to them all. When you pray to one of them, you pray to them all.

Most of us are naturally more drawn to one person of the Trinity than to another. And there are also certain occasions during our lives when we may feel the need of God's presence in a particular way. Perhaps the chaos and the suffering of the Thirty Years War created a particular need for the personal presence of the second person of the Trinity: Jesus, who in the midst of want and gloom, death and tomb, was a faithful and loving companion and filled the heart with joy.

While we may naturally prefer one or the other because of our various temperaments, we are wise if we learn to move among all these spiritualities. We need to be able to sing equally heartily to the Creator, to the Son, and to the Holy Spirit. We need to learn to pray in many ways: in the name of the Creator who brought the world into being, in the name of the Spirit who moves among us, and in the name of Jesus, who brings us the gladness of close and constant friendship.

Proper 6: *The Sunday closest to June 15*

Hymn 528   Lord, you give the great commission
Jeffery Rowthorn (b.1934)

Jeffery Rowthorn (see Hymn 394, Sixth Sunday of Easter) wrote this strong hymn during his years at Yale. It first appeared in *Laudamus* (1980), a hymnal supplement for use in daily worship at Yale Divinity School.

The text is based on sayings from the Gospels of Matthew and Luke. Each stanza begins with the salutation "Lord," followed by a description of God's call to us, and then a prayer that we may respond to that call. Finally the refrain invokes the Holy Spirit to empower us as we respond.

The following Scriptural passages are incorporated, in part or in whole, in the text:

1. "As you go, proclaim the good news, 'The kingdom of heaven has come near.'" (Mt.10:7)
"Cure the sick, raise the dead, cleanse the lepers, cast out demons." (Mt.10:8)
2. "Go therefore and make disciples of all nations,

baptizing them in the name of the Father and of the Son and of the Holy Spirit." (Mt. 28:19)

3. "While they were eating, Jesus took a loaf of bread, and after blessing it broke it, gave it to the disciples, and said, 'Take, eat; this is my body.' Then he took a cup, and after giving thanks he gave it to them, saying 'Drink from it, all of you; for this is my blood of the covenant, which is poured out for many for the forgiveness of sins.'" (Mt. 26:26–28)

4. "Then Jesus said, 'Father, forgive them; for they do not know what they are doing.'" (Lk. 23:34)

5. "And remember, I am with you always, to the end of the age." (Mt. 28:20)

The hymn text was set to music by Alec Wyton, whom Jeffery Rowthorn had met while both were teaching at Union Theological Seminary in New York City.

୧୨

Ministry is the work of all of God's people, both lay and ordained. When we are baptized, each of us is called to "proclaim by word and example the Good News of God in Christ," to "seek and serve Christ in all persons," and to "strive for justice and peace."

In doing this work, we all have to face the same problem: how can we "do ministry" without falling prey to burnout, egotism, or hypocrisy?

Jeffery Rowthorn's hymn reminds us of the right order of things.

First, our ministry is a *response*, and not our own initiative. Jesus' voice calls from the Gospels: "Heal the sick and preach the word"; "In my name baptize and teach"; "This is my body, this my blood"; "Father, what they do, forgive."

When we are in a dilemma about what God wants us to do, Jesus' words help point the way. Does it involve in some way the work of healing, preaching, welcoming into community, teaching, gathering to break bread, and forgiving? Does it use our own special gifts, help them to grow, and give us an opportunity to share them with others? Does it help to mend the world?

Secondly, the source—and the energy—of all ministry is prayer; it is prayer that guides us, and prayer that sustains us. Indeed, prayer alone can be ministry. But above all, to plunge into activity without prayer is to invite exhaustion.

And yet, the more important and urgent our work of ministry seems to us, the more we are likely to be tempted to skip those moments we spend with God. We rush off to a meeting, or decide to make a few telephone calls, thinking we'll attend to prayer later in the day, when we have a "break." But somehow, that break never comes, and we find ourselves frazzled and fragmented, and wonder why.

If we claim our time with God as the very source of our ability to do ministry, we will begin each day with whatever way of prayer feeds our souls. Perhaps it will be meditation on Scripture or on the events in our appointment book for that day; perhaps it will be sitting silently, breathing in God's *ruach*; perhaps, even it will be some of the words of this hymn:

"Help us witness to your purpose with renewed integrity . . . give us all new fervor, draw us closer in community . . . .may your care and mercy lead us to a just society . . . may we serve as you intend, and . . . hold in mind eternity." Amen!

That is the right sequence of things: to respond, to pray, and, finally, to do. We don't try to do our work without God's sustenance any more than we would venture forth on a long automobile trip with an empty gas tank. And we can't produce the fuel ourselves: we ask God's Spirit to flow through us and to help us accept Jesus' invitation to do his work in the world.

Proper 7: The Sunday closest to June 22

Hymn 445, 446   Praise to the Holiest in the height
John Henry Newman (1801–1890)

John Henry Newman—theologian, reformer, and author—was a major figure in English ecclesiastical history.

Ordained in 1824, he became vicar in 1828 of St. Mary's, the University Church at Oxford. Along with Keble and Pusey, he was a leader of the Oxford Movement, also known as the Tractarian Movement because of the *Tracts for the Times* (many written by Newman) which the group began to publish in 1834. The movement was to influence the Church of England in many ways: in the sphere of worship and ceremonial, in a higher regard for the ministry, in a renewed emphasis on work among the poor, and in the founding of religious communities.

After a prolonged inner struggle, Newman was received into the Roman Catholic Church in 1845 and was ordained priest in Rome in 1846. Back in England in 1847, he organized the Oratory of St. Philip Neri in Birmingham, where he lived in semi-seclusion with some of his followers. Because of his keen mind, he was appointed rector of the newly organized and short-lived Dublin Catholic University, where he served from 1854 to 1858. During that time, he wrote the educational classic *The Idea of a University*. His autobiography, *Apologia pro Vita Sua* (*Apology for His Life*), published in 1864, won wide public sympathy. In 1877 he was elected an Honorary Fellow of Trinity College, and two years later Pope Leo XIII elevated him to the College of Cardinals.

Newman's masterpiece is considered by many to be his epic poem, "The Dream of Gerontius," written in 1865 and later made famous by the oratorio of Sir Edward Elgar. Written during a period of personal crisis and life-threatening illness, the poem is a meditation on the progress of an individual soul through death, while conversing with an accompanying angel. Their discourse is repeatedly interrupted, first by concerted demons, then by five choirs of angels that sing in turn, always beginning with what is now known as the first stanza of "Praise to the Holiest in the height."

The stanzas that make up the hymn are sung by the "Fifth Choir of Angelicals," leading Percy Dearmer to remark, "Very soon, thanks to the Dykes tune, it was being sung by most choirs of evangelicals also and appeared in many hymn books."[68] The second tune was composed in 1912 for Newman's text by Richard Runciman Terry, Director of Music at the Roman Catholic Westminster Cathedral, London.

ↄ৹

What a contrast "Praise to the Holiest in the height" provides to some of the subjective hymns we have considered! It is a text of pure praise, directed entirely towards God. There is no mention of "I" or "me" or "my." The singer seems to lose all sense of self in this paean of adoration.

The music of the angelic chorus is described by the "Soul" in Newman's poem as a sound

like the rushing of the wind—
The summer wind—among the lofty pines;
Swelling and dying, echoing round about,
Now here, now distant, wild and beautiful;
While, scatter'd from the branches it has stirr'd,
Descend ecstatic odours.
. . . a grand mysterious harmony:
It floods me, like the deep and solemn sound
Of many waters.[69]

The angels echo all creation in glorifying God.

Praise is the angels' "work," their vocation. It isn't a mindless "praise God," or a "positive attitude," or the mere recitation of a litany. The angels shine with their praise; their golden voices reverberate throughout all creation.

Praise is our vocation, too. When we direct our attention entirely upon God, we become our most true selves.

Some of us have learned about that paradox through more humble examples. When I was young, I was always shy and very uncomfortable if I had to speak in public. I remember, as a young teacher, losing my self-consciousness as I became totally absorbed in my work with children. Forgetting myself gave me a freedom I had never known before.

Many of us have known what it means to be totally enwrapped in what we are experiencing, and to emerge from those moments with a renewed sense of who we are. Perhaps it was great music, great art, or great drama that lured us from our accustomed egocentricity. Perhaps it was the experience of gazing into the Grand Canyon or observing a meteor shower on an August night. We may lose ourselves—and find ourselves—in our love for another human being: a spouse, a child, a parent, or a friend. Or perhaps it is our work—writing a book, playing a violin, planting a garden, serving our community, tending the sick, building a house —that bestows the gift of self-forgetfulness.

Perhaps that is our life's agenda: learning to lose ourselves so that in the end we can find ourselves.

Jesus, after all, "lost himself" to find us: "Christ Jesus, who though he was in the form of God, did not regard equality with God as something to be exploited, but emptied himself. . . ."

We can turn that around and say that losing ourselves is a way to find God: not hating ourselves, or devaluing ourselves, but forgetting ourselves for a moment, or maybe for a lifetime.

Proper 8: The Sunday closest to June 29

Hymn 572   Weary of all trumpeting
Martin H. Franzmann (1907–1976)

This is one of those rare hymns in which the tune inspired the text, rather than the reverse. In the late 1930s, Hitler's Third Reich enlisted the help of poets to help extol the virtues of Germany's annexation of Austria. They assigned one of these texts to the gifted composer and church musician, Hugo Distler. Distler, who was hostile to the Nazi regime, obeyed under duress. The result was a melody that is tinged with sadness rather than triumph. The song was printed on a postcard (of which only one remains) and sold. Distler, distressed by the horrors of war, the deaths of his friends, and the threat of military service in a cause he abhorred, was finally to commit suicide in 1942.

Distler's composition student and friend Jan Bender kept the tune in his mind during the subsequent years and in 1965 wrote *Variations for Organ on a Theme by Hugo Distler*. He continued, however, to believe that it deserved a suitable text.

He finally commissioned Martin Franzmann to write a poem for Distler's tune. It is a welcome irony that Franzmann produced an anti-war text for the tune originally written to celebrate one of Hitler's victories.

Franzmann, born in Minnesota and educated in Wisconsin, Missouri, and Illinois, was a highly regarded preacher and teacher of the Lutheran Church-Missouri Synod. Over the years, he served on many official and doctrinal commissions of his church. He went to England in 1969 to teach at a Lutheran study center in Cambridge; the surprise discovery was made that he had never been ordained, and he was ordained into the Evangelical Lutheran Church of England. After a few years in Cambridge, he retired to Wells, Somerset. The author of biblical, theological, and devotional books, he began translating German hymns in the late 1930s and also began writing his own original hymns about the same time.

"Weary of all trumpeting," a poem of what Erik Routley has described as "rough-cast ruggedness,"[70] is typical of Franzmann's distinctive style.

❦

I would venture to say we are all weary of wars, no matter what our political stance on the subject. Those of us who follow the Prince of Peace cannot help but ache inside when violence kills and maims human beings and destroys not only cities but the natural environment. But what can we do about it?

We can build a cathedral, for one thing. On the night of Thursday, November 14, 1940, enemy bombs destroyed the fourteenth-century Cathedral of St. Michael in Coventry. Eventually there rose beside the ruins a new cathedral, a witness both to the horrors of war and the power of reconciliation.

The new cathedral is bathed in the reds, blues, and golds of the great stained glass window behind a font fashioned from a boulder from the hills of Bethlehem, where the shepherds heard the angels' message of peace on earth. Beyond the high altar hangs a brilliant tapestry depicting the risen Christ enthroned in glory. But there is a subtheme to the message of peace and resurrection, one that is suggested by the wrought-iron crown of thorns that forms the gate to the Gethsemane Chapel, by the cross of iron nails cradled by the silver and gold High Altar Cross, and by the bust of Christ crucified sculpted from the debris of a wrecked automobile: the theme of suffering.

When you step outside the new Coventry cathedral, you find yourself face to face with the devastation of war. You are in the old cathedral, now roofless and ruined, its useless windows a filigree against the sky. There, behind a rough altar, stands a cross made from great charred beams which fell from the roof that dreadful November night, with a reredos, not of Christ in Glory, but of a simple carved prayer: "FATHER FORGIVE."

The Cathedral of St. Michael at Coventry teaches me about dealing with the violence that is so pervasive in our modern world, whether it takes the form of bloodshed in ethnic civil wars faraway or in gang slayings in city streets in our own country.

It reminds me that both the potential for resurrection

and the capacity for warfare lurk in us all. It reminds me that, no matter how carefully we construct our lives, we all have the capacity to do harm to others.

How do we work for peace? The most effective beginning is to become people of peace. And the first step is to acknowledge that we ourselves need God's help and forgiveness.

When we do that, we will begin to see our so-called enemies, whether they live a continent away, or down the street, as fellow human beings, flawed as we are. When we have forgiven ourselves, through God's grace, for being the complex and unruly creatures that we are, we will be able to pray the prayer of Coventry: "Father, forgive." And, if enough of us, "weary of all trumpeting," do that, perhaps God's intended reign of peace will eventually bless our world.

Independence Day   *July 4*

Hymn 594, 595   God of grace and God of glory
Harry Emerson Fosdick (1878–1969)

Harry Emerson Fosdick was born in Buffalo, New York, received a B.A. from Colgate University, a B.Div. from Union Theological Seminary, and a M.A. from Columbia University. He was ordained as a Baptist minister in 1903, served as pastor in the First Baptist Church in Montclair, New Jersey, and was appointed professor of practical theology at Union Seminary in 1915. During World War I, he spent six months visiting soldiers overseas under the auspices of the YMCA and the British Ministry of Information. While at Union, he became a regular "guest preacher" at the First Presbyterian Church in New York until fundamentalist pressure caused him to be expelled from its pulpit because of his liberal views. At this point, John D. Rockefeller invited him to become the pastor of the Park Avenue Baptist Church. At first, Fosdick declined, commenting that Mr. Rockefeller was "too wealthy," to which Rockefeller replied, "Do you think more people will criticize you on account of my wealth than will criticize me on account of your heresy?" Fosdick finally decided to accept, laying down certain conditions, including the provision that a new church be built in "a less swank district."

Soon thereafter Riverside Church was built on Morningside Heights, providing a wide and interdenominational ministry for Fosdick. From its pulpit, he preached to enormous congregations and reached millions of others by means of his more than thirty-two books and his "National Vespers" radio broadcasts. An early supporter of pastoral counselling and of the church's cooperation with psychiatry, he became one of the most influential twentieth-century interpreters of religious belief and thought in America.

His popular hymn "God of grace and God of glory" was written at Fosdick's summer home at Boothbay Harbor, Maine. It was sung for the opening service of Riverside Church on October 5, 1930, and again at the dedication service on February 8, 1931. The text inspired the title of Fosdick's autobiography *The Living of These Days* (1956).

Fosdick conceived of the text as being sung to the tune REGENT SQUARE and was not happy when it soon was sung to other tunes. In *The Hymnal 1982*, the two choices are a Welsh tune with which the text is ecumenically associated and a tune, by a nineteenth century American composer, first paired with the text in *The Hymnal 1940*.

❧

When we meditate on the evil in the world, it is tempting to believe that one person can do nothing to change things. To avoid "weak resignation," we need reminders from people like the admissions officer of my college who created a poster with the motto: "Think one person can change the world? So do we." Since I have come back to live in the town where that college is located, I have become friends with many students. I admire their energetic idealism—sometimes to the point of contentiousness—and their willingness to put themselves on the line for justice. I fervently hope that they are typical of the young people about to be launched into the world from all our institutions of higher learning.

Harry Emerson Fosdick would have fit right in here. He preached a "social Gospel" from the pulpit at Riverside Church: the "good news" that the Christian ought to change the world. This was no easy optimism; change is always hard-won, and the church would need wisdom and courage in its struggle against the hosts of evil. Her people would first need to be transformed themselves: from proud and selfish people, "rich in things and poor in soul," to brave, informed warriors of peace.

Those of us within the church often underestimate the power we have in the eyes of the world. But it is a reality that was brought home to me recently through an interesting sequence of events. I had become concerned about a proposal for a cargo jetport in our rural county that would destroy the quality of life for those who lived nearby; it was an issue both of social justice and of environmental stewardship. I wrote to the county commissioner and got a prompt telephone call inviting me to come to meet with him, with any friends I would like to bring along.

It was only when I issued the first invitation to a friend,

and he looked at me with disbelief, that I found out how extraordinary the commissioner's response to me had been. My friend, a public official himself, had been trying to get the commissioner's ear for weeks about the same issue, but had failed. As we discussed the mystery of why the commissioner had responded to me so promptly, we both realized that perhaps it was because he had spied "The Rev." at the top of my stationery.

My friends and I did meet with the commissioner, and a "town meeting" was planned, to which over 150 upset people came. Before our meeting, the commissioner had heard only those special interest groups who hoped to gain financially from the proposed plan. But now the commissioner heard the voices of his constituents, and we are hoping that the issue is a dead one.

One little letter with "The Rev." at the top! It made me realize that the church has power, and we might as well use that power for God's purposes. Think one Christian can change the world? I think so! For that person represents something greater: the power on earth of the church community, strengthened by the eternal power of God.

Proper 9: The Sunday closest to July 6

Hymn 302, 303   Father, we thank thee who hast planted
Greek, ca. 110; tr. *F. Bland Tucker (1895–1984)*

Our oldest Christian hymn text is from an early second-century Egyptian or Syrian document known as the *Didache*, or "teaching." It is a practical, "how-to" book, containing both a code of Christian morals, presented as a choice between the way of life and the way of death, and a manual of church order. In the manual of church order are simple rules for the conduct of a rural congregation concerning baptism, fasting, itinerant prophets, and the local ministry of bishops and deacons. Its antiquity is revealed especially in its closing paragraph, a warning about the approaching end of the world.

"Father, we thank thee who hast planted" is a paraphrase of several of the Eucharistic prayers in the *Didache*, which are modeled on Jewish forms for grace before and after meals, and may even pre-date the document which contains them. It is clear that, for this community who believed they were living during the "last days," the Lord's Supper was a joyful and expectant Messianic Banquet.

Now as regards the Eucharist (the Thank-offering), give thanks after this manner: First for the cup: "We give thanks to you, our Father, for the holy vine of David your servant, which you have made known to us through Jesus, your servant; to you be the glory for ever." And for the broken bread: "We give thanks to you, our Father, for the life and knowledge which you have made known to us through Jesus, Thy servant: to you be the glory for ever. As this broken bread was scattered over the hills, and then was brought together and made one, so let your Church be brought together from the ends of the earth into your Kingdom. . . . We thank you, holy Father, for your sacred name which you had lodged in our hearts, and for the knowledge and faith and immortality which you have revealed through Jesus, your child. . . . You, O Almighty Sovereign, made all things for your Name's sake; you gave food and drink to men for enjoyment that they might give thanks to You; but to us you did freely give spiritual food and drink and eternal life through your servant. . . . Remember, Lord, your Church, to save it from all evil and to make it perfect by your love. Make it holy, and gather it, together from the four winds, into your Kingdom which you have made ready for it. For yours is the power and the glory forever. Let Grace come and let this world pass away. Hosanna to the God of David! If anyone is holy, let him come. If not, let him repent. Maranatha! [Our Lord, come!] Amen."[71]

The text can be sung either to a sixteenth-century Genevan psalter tune, or to a contemporary setting by an American.

❧

Praying this text transports us back in time to a young church living in a dangerous age, when it was risky to meet on every "Lord's Day—his special day." But coming together was of utmost importance, so that one could confess one's sins, give thanks, and break bread, in the community which was Christ's body on earth.

The sense of community which we struggle to achieve today was natural for these desert ancestors, for they came from a tradition in which belonging was of prime importance. Being ostracized from one's people was the ultimate shame, which was why it was so shocking to pious Jews when Jesus hobnobbed with lepers, tax-collectors, and other outcasts of society.

Today it is the individual rather than the community who takes pride of place in our culture. The shadow side of that emphasis is loneliness. And loneliness is why many people are drawn to churches, hoping for the fellowship promised by coffee hours, rummage sales, and pot luck suppers.

However, the ultimate sign of community is found, not around well-laden tables in the parish hall, but around the altar, in a simple meal of bread and wine. It is that simple meal, rather than all the busy-ness of "fellowship," which really teaches us how to be community.

That meal tells us that our community is like the bread we share. We were many grains of wheat, gathered from the various hillsides which are our ethnic and social backgrounds. The yeast of Jesus' spirit, the water and oil of grace, and the kneading of our work together make us into one loaf. A collection of individuals become more than the sum of all its parts: like rising bread in a warm corner of the kitchen, we grow into community.

We are not meant merely to maintain our community, because that is a recipe for becoming stale. Instead, we are broken and shared, like the good bread from the altar. For we are meant to feed others through our ministry—to feed them in all kinds of ways.

As we attend to the business of ministry, we put into God's hands the task of maintenance. "Watch o'er thy Church, O Lord, in mercy." While we need to be wise as serpents and gentle as doves regarding the inevitable sins and schisms which arise wherever there is human nature at work, unity—and community—happens, again and again, as we reenact the simple task of gathering, thanking, breaking, and sharing our gifts with the world around us.

Proper 10: *The Sunday closest to July 13*

Hymn 588, 589   Almighty God, your word is cast
John Cawood (1775–1852)

John Cawood was born in Derbyshire, England. His family were farmers on a small scale; their extremely modest income meant that Cawood received a very limited childhood education. At the age of eighteen, he entered into menial service to the Rev. Mr. Cursham, a clergyman in Nottinghamshire. After studying for three years under the private tutelage of the Rev. Edward Spencer, rector of Wingfield, Wiltshire, however, he entered St. Edmund's Hall, Oxford. He received a Bachelor of Arts degree in 1801 and was ordained the same year. Six years later, he received a Master of Arts degree.

Cawood served as curate to adjacent parishes of Ribbesford and Dowles, and in 1814 became the incumbent of St. Anne's Chapel of Ease, Bewdley, where he remained until his death in 1852.

Written in 1815, "Almighty God, thy word is cast," in its original six-stanza form, was first published in Thomas Cotterill's *A Selection of Psalms and Hymns for Public and Private Use*, eighth edition (1819), with the heading "After Sermon." The text is based on the parable of the sower, found in Mt.13:3–9, Mk.4:3–9, and Lk.8:5–8. In the parable, the sower sowed seeds on a path, where the birds came and devoured them; some fell on rocky ground, where they wilted because they could not put down roots; and some fell among thorns, which choked the young plants. Finally, some fell on good soil, and "yielded a hundredfold."

Both tunes provided are by American composers: the first is in the form of a classic strophic song, and the second contains a melodic motif reminiscent of a peal of bells.

&

From the earliest Christian hymn in our hymnal (see Hymn 302, 303, Proper 9) to the present day, poets have used the image of planting and growing to suggest the abundant life God offers us.

After all, it is, ultimately, only the amazing process of a plant's growth that feeds us. Without the swelling of the seed, the downward thrust of the roots, the reaching upwards toward the sun, humanity would starve. We are utterly dependent on the process.

In our early history as a species, we gathered what we needed from field and forest—grain, berries, nuts, herbs, fruits—and hunted animals who had done the same. But at some point in time, our ancestors invented agriculture: the deliberate cultivation of what they needed to sustain them.

As they experimented with agriculture, they discovered some rules: a plant needs good soil, water, and sunlight to be able to flourish. And it must be protected from predators and weeds. Growing it is, sometimes, a lot of work.

When Jesus told the story of the sower, he knew very well that nature, being part of the Creator's design, would provide a wise pattern for the lives of those who would follow his Way. So it is no surprise that the parable of the sower provides some good advice about both tilling and tending the soul. In fact, all three writers of the synoptic Gospels include comments after the parable about the story's application to the lives of the hearers.

What is the seed God wants to plant in our hearts, the

seed from which an abundant life will grow? I think that the seed is the potential for love: love of God, love of ourselves as God's creation, and love of others.

Will we let it be snatched away, or trampled by the forces that militate against love? We do that when we reject love in favor of one of the negative ideals our culture often holds out to us: a selfish individualism, arrogant desire for power, or idolatry of earthly wealth.

Will we make it possible for love to put down roots, by providing the deep soil of prayer and reflection? Or will our religion, and probably our lives, be shallow and unfruitful?

Will we be willing to weed out of our lives those things that strangle our potential to grow: our overbusy-ness, our resentments, our thoughtlessness, our sin? In the garden, this is often the most difficult of our tasks, and it requires constant vigilance. In my garden, at least, weeds seem to spring up overnight!

Or will we cultivate our garden? The Sun is overhead, providing free energy. For the garden is a partnership: between the gardener and nature, our soul's work and God's gift. In that partnership, the rays of grace are the indispensable ingredient. We are drawn to God, growing in love and towards Love. It is a labor of love to do our part, as well.

Proper 11: *The Sunday closest to July 20*

Hymn 596   Judge eternal, throned in splendor
Henry Scott Holland (1847–1918)

Henry Scott Holland was born in Hereford, and educated at Eton and at Balliol College, Oxford. Ordained deacon in 1872 and priest in 1874, he became a fellow and select preacher at Oxford, and then canon and precentor at St. Paul's, London, where his skill as a musician contributed to the improvement of musical standards in the cathedral's services. The University of Aberdeen honored him with a Doctor of Divinity degree in 1903, and he returned to Oxford as Regius Professor of Divinity in 1911, remaining there until his death.

Holland was a contributor to *Lux Mundi,* an influential collection of essays by liberal scholars. He was the author also of *So as by fire; notes on the war* (1916), *Our place in Christendom* (1916), and *A Bundle of Memories* (1915), a collection of sermons and autobiographical material.

Because of his deep concern about social problems, Holland was a founder and strong supporter of the Christian Social Union and editor of its magazine *The Commonwealth.*

"Judge eternal, throned in splendor," Holland's only hymn, appeared in the July 1902 issue of *The Commonwealth.* Four years later, it was included in *The English Hymnal,* which he helped to edit. The text embodies the two chief interests of his fruitful life—social reform and missionary work.

A memorial tablet in his honor at Christ Church Cathedral in Oxford bears the words, *Invisibilem tanquam videns*

Deum, Regnum Ejus coeleste fide inconcussa, spe vivida, caritate hilari, nunquam non in terra praestruebat ("As beholding God Invisible, he was unceasingly founding on earth His Heavenly Kingdom, in unshaken faith, lively hope, joyous love.")[72]

The text of Holland's hymn is set to a German hymn tune from the late seventeenth century.

ᴄᴏ

"Judge eternal, throned in splendor" was written in England almost one hundred years ago, but the prayer could well be on the lips of every person in the world today. Still "the weary folk are pining for the hour that brings release, and the city's crowded clangor cries aloud for sin to cease." And, with even more urgency than in Holland's day, today "the homesteads and the woodlands plead in silence for their peace."

What has happened to the peace of the homesteads and the woodlands since Holland wrote his hymn? The scientists who drafted the 1992 manifesto, "Preserving and Cherishing the Earth; an Appeal for Joint Commitment in Science and Religion," can provide the answer:

> The Earth is the birthplace of our species and, so far as we know, our only home. When our numbers were small and our technology feeble, we were powerless to influence the environment of our world. But today, suddenly, almost without anyone noticing, our numbers have become immense and our technology has achieved vast, even awesome powers. Intentionally or inadvertently, we are now able to make devastating changes in the global environment. . . .
>
> We are now threatened by self-inflicted, swiftly moving environmental alterations about whose long-

term biological and ecological consequences we are still painfully ignorant—depletion of the protective ozone layer, a global warming unprecedented in the last 150 millennia; the obliteration of an acre of forest every second; the rapid-fire extinction of species. . . .

By their very nature these assaults on the environment were not caused by any one political group or any one generation. Intrinsically, they are transnational, transgenerational, and transideological. So are all conceivable solutions. . . .

As on issues of peace, human rights, and social justice, religious institutions can here too be a strong force encouraging national and international initiatives in both the private and public sectors, and in the diverse worlds of commerce, education, culture, and mass communication.

The environmental crisis requires radical changes not only in public policy, but also in individual behavior. The historical record makes clear that religious teaching, example and leadership are powerfully able to influence personal conduct and commitment.[73]

So . . . where is the church? Are we answering the call to be a strong force in the nation and the world? Are we teaching our people about how their behavior affects the vanishing woodlands, the warming of the atmosphere, and the weary folk in other parts of the world who have use of only a minuscule proportion of the resources we squander?

May God cleave our darkness with a sword, so that we can be cleansed of indifference and apathy, and help to purge our world of the bitter things that threaten to bring an end to life on earth.

Proper 12: *The Sunday closest to July 27*

Hymn 677   God moves in a mysterious way
William Cowper (1731–1800)

William Cowper was the elder son of the rector of Great Berkhamsted in Hertfordshire and chaplain to George II. His mother, whom he idolized, died when Cowper was six years of age. He was educated at a private school—where he was bullied—and at Westminster, and was called to the bar in 1754, but never practiced. Sensitive and hypochondriac by nature, he began to suffer from severe depression, and when he was offered a position as clerk in the House of Lords, his dread of appearing before the House for the required examination caused him to break down completely and attempt suicide. After some time at a hospital at St. Alban's, the melancholy passed away temporarily, and he turned increasingly to evangelical Christianity for consolation.

When Cowper moved to Huntingdon to be near his brother John, who was at Cambridge, he met the Reverend Morely Unwin, with whose family he became lifelong friends. He soon became a boarder (in Cowper's words, "a sort of adopted son") in their home. When Unwin died in 1767, Cowper met the evangelical John Newton, who came to give his condolences.

Cowper and Unwin's widow moved to Olney, where Newton had a curacy; Cowper worked with Newton as a lay assistant, visiting the parishioners and collaborating with Newton in the publication of *Olney Hymns* (1779), one of the literary masterpieces in the history of hymnody. Cowper contributed sixty-eight original hymns to this distinguished volume.

His long poem *The Task*, published in 1785, brought great success, as did his translation of Homer, and he began to be regarded as the finest poet of his day. However, Mrs. Unwin's death in 1706 brought a recurrence of his malady from which he did not recover, and he died in April 1800.

"God moves in a mysterious way" was first published anonymously in Newton's *Twenty-six Letters on Religious Subjects* (1774), where it was subtitled "Light shining out of Darkness." It was later credited to Cowper in *Olney Hymns*.

The text, with its Scottish psalm tune, is included as a congregational hymn in Benjamin Britten's cantata *Saint Nicolas* (1948).

ↄ∕ↄ

Scott Peck begins his popular book, *The Road Less Traveled*, with the sentence "Life is difficult."[74] Cowper would have agreed with all his heart. But life was made even more difficult for him than was necessary by his unswerving conviction that his problems were visited upon him by Providence. His mother's death, the bullying of his classmates, and his extreme self-consciousness, all were thought by him to be part of God's plan, unfathomable and mysterious. There was a reason for everything; one had only to wait to find out what it was. The dark mines would release their treasure; the ominous clouds would bring welcome rain and sunshine would flood the world. And the God who made these things happen to a six-year-old boy and a fragile young man would one day smile upon him again.

Cowper's God plants "his footsteps in the sea, and rides upon the storm": he is the omnipotent manipulator of events in this world. The poet, struggling with the age-old problem of why evil exists, answers that suffering only masks the good that will eventually come: "Behind a frowning providence [God] hides a smiling face."

I find Cowper's theology deeply disturbing, and do not wonder at his attempts at suicide. What silver lining could there be to the death of his young mother, or to a timidity that forever prevented him from entering into a profession for which he had carefully prepared?

However, as in most theologies, there are embedded within Cowper's some germs of truth. We are, indeed, not in control of life's design; we have a limited perspective on life's events; and God does "move in a mysterious way." But the way is not the way of control, but the way of assistance: helping us to bring new life out of the deaths, real and metaphorical, that come our way. But that is a very different thing from asserting that God controls the world like a cosmic puppeteer, testing us and eventually rewarding the good and punishing the sinner!

Perhaps the best arena in which to test our theology concerning the difficulties of life is in a hospital. On my hospital visits, I hear two kinds of reactions by patients: "The Lord must be punishing me," and "The Lord is with me."

I wish Cowper could have understood that the second is, in the long run, God's mysterious way. God's love surrounds us, whether we deserve it or not, through all the inevitable difficulties of life. Among the wonders of life, this one is the most amazing, and the most comforting.

Proper 13: *The Sunday closest to August 3*

Hymn 320   Zion, praise thy Savior, singing
Att. *Thomas Aquinas (1225?–1274)*

Thomas Aquinas was born into a noble Italian family and was educated in grammar, logic, and philosophy at the Benedictine Abbey at Monte Cassino and the University of Naples. He entered the new Dominican Order of Preachers and soon went to Paris to teach theology.

It was an age of intellectual ferment. Aristotle's works had recently been discovered, and there was much discussion about the impact of Aristotle's emphasis on knowledge derived from reason and sense perception on traditional catholic doctrine, which emphasized faith and revelation. In his great works, the *Summa Theologica* and the *Summa Contra Gentiles*, Thomas asserted that a synthesis of reason and revelation was possible. He was considered a radical thinker, and certain aspects of his thought were condemned by the ecclesiastical authorities. Thomas's canonization less than fifty years after his death vindicated him.

"Zion, praise thy Savior, singing," or *Lauda, Sion, salvatorem*, is a sequence commissioned by Pope Urban VI in 1264 for the newly established Feast of Corpus Christi, a holy day honoring the Eucharist. (Sequences were texts provided for the long vocalizations over the final vowel of the "Alleluia" sung before the Gospel.) Theologians in the eleventh century had been discussing the question of how the bread and wine of the Eucharist could be understood as becoming the body and blood of Christ. By this time, the church had established the doctrine of transubstantiation: the teaching that the outward appearance of the bread and wine remains the same, while the actual substance changes to body and blood.

Lauda, Sion, salvatorem was attributed to Thomas Aquinas by his confessor, Ptolemy of Lucca, in his *Historia ecclesiastica nova* of 1317. The theology and literary quality of the work support that claim, although it is possible that Thomas edited the material from earlier sources. Other hymns in *The Hymnal 1982* written for Corpus Christi and attributed to Thomas are the Vespers hymn *Pange lingua* ("Now my tongue the mystery telling," Hymn 329); and the hymn for Lauds, *Verbum supernum* (of which the final two stanzas are in Hymn 310 and 311: "O saving Victim, opening wide"). Hymn 314, "Humbly I adore thee, Verity unseen" (*Adoro devote*) is also attributed to Thomas.

The plainsong setting, dating from about the year 1100 and originally used for another text, was matched with *Lauda, Sion, salvatorem* ("Zion, praise thy Savior") in the thirteenth century. In 1545–1563, The Council of Trent took upon itself the task of reforming the Roman Catholic Church in response to the Protestant Reformation, and simplified the liturgy by reducing the church's vast repertory of sequences—most of which by that time had become extremely elaborate—to four. "Zion, praise thy Savior, singing" was, fortunately, one that survived.

જી

We need to eat. Food sustains our life. What we eat provides our energy, and, through the miracles of biochemistry, eventually becomes our flesh, our bones, our blood.

The act of eating is basic to human experience, from the

first sweet drops of milk we eagerly suckle as infants, to our ravenous adolescent appetites and our adult savoring of gourmet cooking. Our memories of taste are powerfully evocative; to this day, drinking espresso coffee transports me to the Paris café where I gathered with friends when I was a student there.

When we don't eat, our bodies tell us. We may feel light-headed and weak; our stomachs may rumble, and we may even feel pain—"hunger pangs."

It is a great gift to us that Jesus chose as a memorial such a basic human need. When the twelve met at the holy table, he told them that the food he shared with them would forever after remind them of that meal and of the events that were soon to follow. What he chose was the staple of the Middle Eastern diet—bread—and the most common beverage of Jesus' day—wine. Nothing fancy, just the ordinary menu.

If you were to imagine arriving on earth from a distant planet and finding yourself in a Christian church on a Sunday morning, you may be able to comprehend how very extra-ordinary this action is. It is extraordinary because it is so ordinary: some people gathering for a simple meal. But in that meal, Christians over the years have known the presence of their Lord.

Over the years, people have argued about how Jesus is present in the bread and the wine. However, from the theological controversies of the Middle Ages through the Protestant Reformation and beyond, no one has denied the fact that he is present. And so, throughout the ages, after all our struggles to understand what is ultimately a mystery, we have responded with thanks. That is why we call this meal the "Eucharist," which is derived from the Greek word for "gratitude."

Whether the meal is served in stark simplicity or with all liturgical pomp and circumstance, it gathers Christians together in obedience to their Lord's command: "Do this in remembrance of me."

It is a command that we follow because we need to eat. We need to build up ourselves, the body of Christ, with the good food of Jesus' presence. We need his Spirit's energy to do Jesus' ministry. We need to satisfy our hunger for him.

Proper 14: The Sunday closest to August 10

Hymn 699   Jesus, Lover of my soul
Charles Wesley (1707–1788)

Charles Wesley was the eighteenth of nineteen children of an Anglican clergyman and his wife. He was educated at Westminster School and at Christ Church, Oxford, where he founded a group nicknamed the "Holy Club" or "Methodists" because of its members' devotion to Bible study, prayer, frequent Communion, and the visitation of prisoners and the sick. Ordained in 1735, Charles sailed the next month to Georgia with his brother John to serve as General Oglethorpe's secretary in the new colony. On board ship they became acquainted with twenty-six Moravians who were also passengers. In his journal on January 25, 1736, John described what happened during one of their meetings on board:

> In the midst of the psalm wherewith their service began, the sea broke over, split the mainsail in pieces, covered the ship and poured in between the decks, as

if the great deep had already swallowed us up. A terrible screaming began among the English. The Germans looked up, and without intermission sang on. I asked one of them afterwards, "Was you not afraid?" He answered, "Thank God, no."[75]

This event obviously left a lasting impression. Returning to England after half a year, Charles' ship encountered another frightening storm, and when they finally reached land, on December 3, 1736, Wesley wrote in his journal, "I knelt down and blessed the Hand that had conducted me through such inextricable mazes." Soon the brothers fell in with the Moravians once again, and on Whitsunday 1738, Charles had an evangelical conversion. A few days later his brother John experienced a similar conversion, recorded in his journal:

> In the evening I went very unwillingly to a society [a meeting of Moravians] in Aldersgate Street, where one was reading Luther's Preface to the *Epistle to the Romans*. About a quarter before nine, while he was describing the change which God works in the heart through faith in Christ, I felt my heart strangely warmed. I felt that I did trust in Christ, Christ alone for salvation; and an assurance was given to me that he had taken away *my* sins, even *mine*, and saved *me* from the jaws of sin and death.[76]

Charles joined his brother John in itinerant preaching, and the brothers—who never left the Church of England—figure jointly in the calendar of the Book of Common Prayer (1979), commemorated together as "priests, poets, and teachers of the faith."

Of all the 6,500 hymns Charles Wesley wrote, this is

generally considered to be his finest. Henry Ward Beecher, noted American preacher of the past century, once wrote,

> I would rather have written that hymn of Wesley's than to have the fame of all the kings that ever sat on earth; it is more glorious, it has more power in it. I would rather be the author of that hymn than to hold the wealth of the richest man in New York. He will die after a little while, pass out of men's thought, what will there be to speak of him? But people will go on singing that hymn until the last trump brings forth the angel band; and then I think it will mount upon some lips to the very presence of God.[77]

The hymn is matched with a strong Welsh tune, common to English-language hymnals around the world.

☙

When I sing this hymn, with its melody like the great roll of the waves, I like to think of Charles Wesley on board ship during the storm described in his brother's journal.

There is something about being in a storm at sea that makes us recognize our helplessness. On land, we can take shelter; but there is no shelter in the primordial vastness of the deep. We are at the mercy of the fierce wind and the rolling waves, hoping that our craft is worthy and our captain skilled.

The ocean is a thing of beauty and also of terror. No wonder that people are perennially fascinated by tales of ocean voyages, from *The Odyssey* and *Moby Dick* to the sinking of the *Titanic*. I sailed to Europe once on a small student ship and remember standing on deck, looking at water extending to the horizon as far as the eye could see.

Air travel has erased that experience of the ocean's vastness for most of us, but, should we have a window seat, we can sometimes see the deep waters below, reminding us.

No wonder that the unpredictability of storms at sea has become a favorite metaphor for the times when we feel buffeted and battered by life's events. When Charles Wesley faced dangerously hostile crowds during his itinerant preaching, he very likely compared those situations to his eventful sea voyage with the Moravians.

Who is our refuge in life's storms? Where is our harbor? Our haven is the heaven of Jesus' presence. It is difficult to miss the common derivation of those very similar words.

The image of water is transformed in the course of the hymn. The angry waters of the ocean are replaced by the healing waters of streams and the fountain of life. These friendlier waters represent God's grace to Wesley.

But I like to think of the image of the ocean as capable of transformation, too. Perhaps the ocean can remind us that, rather than always seeking refuge from the storms of life, we can find God in them. God need not be just a healing stream or a gentle fountain. God can be the ocean, too.

The ocean of God is vast and uncharted territory. But we do know some things about the way God acts in the world.

There are wonders in the depths of the ocean that are accessible only to the deep-sea diver's—or the saint's or the mystic's—eye. Not being deep-sea divers, we often look only on the turbulent surface of events when they trouble us, but do not realize that fathoms below that surface is another world, unseen.

And our gaze is so limited! We can't even imagine what lies beyond the sea's wide horizons. The ocean is the domain of the unknown and of mystery.

And yet it is there, supporting us. When I swim in the surf, I have learned that, if I permit it, the sea carries me. Sometimes I float on a calm sea. Sometimes the waves are strong, and they can be frightening. But I have learned not to fight them. They will continue to carry me if I do not struggle.

Jesus walked on the waves towards a small boat in the Sea of Galilee to comfort his frightened disciples caught in a storm. The sea supported him. And the sea that is God will carry us, too, and we will discover, perhaps, that we will need to find no other refuge or haven, but can just rest in that truth.

Proper 15: The Sunday closest to *August 17*

Hymn 469, 470   There's a wideness in God's mercy
Frederick William Faber (1814–1863)

Frederick William Faber was born into a strict Calvinist family whose ancestors had been Huguenots for generations. During his years at Balliol College in Oxford, he attended services at St. Mary's and soon became an enthusiastic admirer of John Henry Newman, then vicar of the church. He threw himself eagerly into the work of the Tractarian Movement and contributed translations of saints' biographies to the publication project.

Elected to a fellowship at University College, Faber set to work preparing himself for ordination in the Anglican Church. During a long vacation, he took a group of friends to Ambleside in the Lake District, and met William Wordsworth, whose poetry he had long admired. In later years, he would describe the long rambles they would take together in the mountains.

Faber traveled on the Continent for much of the next four years, during which time his feelings about the Roman Catholic Church began to change. When he returned, he became vicar of a small parish in Huntingdonshire. During an evening service, in his third year there, he explained to his congregation that his personal convictions had led him to seek admission into the Roman Catholic Church, and that he must leave them.

He was admitted into the Roman Catholic Church the next day. Rebaptized as Father Wilfred, he founded a community known as the Brothers of the Will of God, later called the Wilfridians. In 1849, they merged with Newman's group, the Oratorians, and Faber was appointed Superior of their London branch. Wealthy supporters provided impressive premises in Brompton: the Brompton Oratory of St. Philip Neri. Despite Faber's duties there, he saw service to the poor as his principal vocation, and he wrote tracts and hymns and conducted parish missions with them in mind. Faber was known as a man of great personal charm, and a preacher with the gift of persuasion.

He is best remembered today for his 150 hymn texts, written to correspond to the number of the psalms. He knew from experience the influence that hymn singing had in Protestant circles, and wanted to provide similar devotional materials for the Roman Catholic Church. His hymns, modeled after the hymns of Cowper, Newton, and Wesley, were written primarily to be read in private.

"There's a wideness in God's mercy" is part of a thirteen-verse poem called "Come to Jesus," composed for the parish missions that Faber conducted in England and Ireland. Most of his hymns are too introspective, emotional, or explicitly Roman Catholic to be suitable for general use, but this one continues to be sung throughout Christendom.

There are two musical settings for Faber's hymn: a plaintive contemporary song with an undulating accompaniment, and a straightforward nineteenth-century tune.

❧

This may be one of the most comforting of all hymns. I have in my possession a small blue-and-gilt bound book, dated 1875, containing *Hymns* by Frederick William Faber, D.D. "With a Sketch of his Life." One of the first illustrations in the book is an etching of a Victorian woman, a book open on her lap, reading beside a leaded casement window. The text underneath tells me that, "from his earliest years, Frederick Faber gave promise of remarkable power of mind, which his parents, who were persons of considerable ability, carefully fostered. Owing to the death of three children immediately preceding him, he was the object of his mother's special affection."[78]

I wonder if Faber's conviction of God's expansive mercy and eternal kindness began at his mother's knee

I suspect that this early experience of love formed his childhood idea of what his heavenly parent was like, an idea that stood him in good stead throughout his life, informing his understanding of faith as a Calvinist, an Anglican, and a Roman Catholic alike.

It is illuminating to read the complete poem from which "There's a wideness in God's mercy" was excerpted, for the poem is not only a song of comfort: it is a challenge as well. Faber writes, in one of the (sadly) omitted stanzas:

But we make His love too narrow
By false limits of our own;
And we magnify His strictness
With a zeal He will not own.

Faber, who moved throughout his life among reformers
and converts, probably often observed the shadow side of
zeal, which is intolerance.

Even with these stanzas omitted, the text challenges us.
If God's mercy is wide, if God's justice is kind, if God wel-
comes sinners, should not we, made in the image of God, do
the same? If God feels the sorrows of earth, should not we?

Yet, in human history, sometimes it has been the most
"religious" people who think that God's mercy, justice, and
forgiveness is limited to those who hold certain theological
views, or live certain life-styles, or have been born into
certain ethnic groups. Look at the Inquisition, for example,
or the subtler religious intolerance that drove so many
people to the shores of the New World, or the factions that
divide Christians today.

When my late mother was preparing to enter a retirement community a few years ago, she had to fill out innu-
merable forms, among them one that was marked "Social."
To make it easier for her to respond to the questions, I read
each one to her. She was not of a generation given to self-
revelation, and some of the answers were difficult to draw
out of her. I doubted that I would get any answer when I got
to the question, "What kind of people don't you like?"
Mother had always accentuated the positive, and I had rarely
heard her say a negative word about anyone. But I had no
sooner finished the question than she responded, without a
moment of hesitation: "People who are narrow."

She knew, from over ninety years of thoughtful living

and praying, that narrowness and intolerance made no more sense than putting limitations on the love of a God whose mercy and kindness are as wide as the sea.

Proper 16: The Sunday closest to August 24

Hymn 525   The Church's one foundation
Samuel John Stone (1839–1900)

This hymn was born out of controversy. Samuel John Stone, a curate in Windsor and later known for his work of ministering to the poor in the East End of London, wrote a series of hymns on the Creed. He published these hymns as *Lyra Fidelium: Twelve Hymns on the Twelve Articles of the Apostles' Creed* (1866). The ninth hymn was "The Church's one foundation," headed "Article XI. The Holy Catholic Church: the Communion of Saints. 'He is the Head of the Body, the Church.'"

The church was, in Stone's view, by "heresies distressed." A certain John William Colenso, the Anglican Bishop of Natal in South Africa, had printed some papers on *The Pentateuch and the Book of Joshua Critically Examined* in 1862. One of the early works of Biblical criticism (in the sense of taking seriously the historical, social, and literary context of the Bible), the papers challenged the traditional view of the Scriptures. Colenso's liberal pastoral policies did not help: he did not insist that Africans who came to him for baptism divorce all their wives except one, and was accused of condoning polygamy. Colenso was accused of "doing sums on the Pentateuch" (he had been a teacher of mathematics at Harrow) and undermining the foundations of the Christian faith. He was deposed from his see by Bishop Gray of Cape Town in 1863; and, though he appealed—and won—his case, Gray's defense of tradition inspired many, including Stone. Despite his legal victory, Colenso was excommunicated in 1866. The controversy continued throughout the church, and the result was the first Lambeth Conference in 1867, where the issue was high on the agenda of the bishops who gathered from the worldwide Anglican Communion.

Throughout the rest of the nineteenth century, other controversies were to arise, such as the challenges of Darwinism. Stone's hymn, which spoke to the anxieties of these times, became increasingly popular.

The third Lambeth Conference was held in 1888, and the Lambeth Quadrilateral (the classic Anglican statement regarding the essence of the Christian faith) was adopted. For this historic meeting, a longer ten-stanza version of Stone's hymn, written originally for processional use at Salisbury Cathedral, was sung as the processional hymn at all the three great services at Canterbury Cathedral, Westminster Abbey, and St.Paul's. Afterwards, Bishop Nelson of New Zealand wrote:

Bard of the Church, in these divided days
For words of harmony to thee we praise:
Of love and oneness thou didst strike the chords,
The Church's one Foundation thou didst sing. . . .[79]

The tune by Samuel Sebastian Wesley, grandson of Charles Wesley, was matched with the text in 1868.

༒

It is thought-provoking to read the story of "The Church's one foundation" and to realize how much our outlook has changed since Bishop Colenso's study of the first six books of the Bible shattered the peace of the church. Today, most of us read the Bible like Colenso, rather than like his adversary, Bishop Gray; we find inspiration in recognizing the Spirit's guidance, not merely in the words which are contained between the bindings of our Old and New Testaments, but in the process of how they got there.

One of my New Testament professors was fond of saying "Jesus lived in the era before videotape." The implication of those words is that the history found in the Scripture was seen through human eyes, rather than through a camera. As we know, when five people are asked to describe the same incident, the result is inevitably five different versions of the story, although each version is the truth as understood by the teller. The complexity grows if each person passes on the story to someone else, and the story is told and retold until finally it is written down.

My professor taught me how to apply that lesson to the Gospels. The task became endlessly fascinating; it changed what the Bible meant to me. As I underlined passages, and wrote notes in the margin, something happened: I rediscovered the power in the stories that had become humdrum from over-familiarity. More than that, this study brought me closer to the Jesus who was the subject of so many stories and so much conjecture among his earliest followers.

For me, approaching the Bible as did Bishop Colenso was an experience of "the Church's one foundation is Jesus Christ her Lord"! I am filled with wonder when I observe the Spirit of Christ in shaping what became the Christian Scripture I hold as a book in my hands.

And the story of this hymn also reminds me that, in our controversies, we can never be absolutely certain that we are standing on God's side. Jesus' life was not recorded on videotape. Nor do we hear present truth from God's loudspeaker. The best we can do is to listen to one another in humility. We may think we are basing our opinions on the foundation of Jesus Christ, but perhaps, instead, we are blocking the work of the Spirit. We can never know, in this life.

Meanwhile, underneath all of us is the Foundation on which we stand—the Lord Jesus who probably smiles at our petty quarrels and eagerly waits for us to enter the church triumphant in eternity.

Proper 17: *The Sunday closest to August 31*

Hymn 654   Day by day
Att. *Richard of Chichester (1197–1253)*

Richard of Chichester was born in Worcestershire; both his parents died when he and his brother were quite young, leaving a rich estate in the hands of a guardian. When the estate dwindled due to mismanagement, Richard worked long hours to restore it. Although pressure was put upon Richard to marry, he turned the estate over to his brother and chose the life of a scholar. At Oxford, under the tutelage of such guides as Robert Grosseteste (who was later to be Bishop of Lincoln), he met with success, despite the fact that he was often hungry and cold. He went to Paris, and then to Bologna, to study law, earned a doctorate, and returned to Oxford around 1235 as University Chancellor.

Shortly thereafter, Edmund, the Archbishop of Canterbury, appointed him as his own chancellor, and a close friendship began between the two men. Edmund's attempt to check the royal exploitation of ecclesiastical wealth and patronage brought him into conflict with King Henry III. The archbishop went into exile in France; Richard accompanied him and nursed him in his final illness. Edmund was canonized in 1247.

After Edmund's death, Richard studied and taught at the Dominican house at Orleans, and was ordained priest in 1243. He returned to England and in 1244 was elected Bishop of Chichester, in the south of England. King Henry, however, favored a rival candidate and opposed the election; he confiscated all the revenues of the diocese and locked Richard out of the episcopal dwelling. A local priest gave him lodging, and he functioned as a missionary bishop. A man of deep spirituality and an excellent administrator, he traveled about the diocese to visit his flock and held synods under the most trying conditions.

Finally, the threats of the Pope persuaded King Henry to acknowledge Richard as Bishop. He was to serve his diocese as preacher, confessor, teacher, and counselor for eight years. While campaigning in 1253 for a new crusade against the Saracens, he contracted a fatal fever. Richard was canonized nine years after his death. His shrine in Chichester Cathedral, where many cures were said to have been wrought, was destroyed by order of Henry VIII in 1538.

The popular musical *Godspell* paid homage—perhaps inadvertently—to St. Richard, by including a song entitled "Day by Day." Like our hymn, it is taken from a prayer believed to be written by Richard, and for which the saint is best remembered:

"Thanks be to thee, O Lord Jesus Christ, for all the benefits which thou hast given us; for all the pains and insults which thou hast borne for us. O most merciful redeemer, friend and brother, may we know thee more clearly, love thee more dearly, and follow thee more nearly; for thine own sake. Amen."

The music, of a contemplative nature, was composed specifically for this text in 1941.

℘

I will never forget an early visit to Chichester Cathedral, when my husband and I joined a group led by one of those knowledgeable and lively guides who magically transform a stroll around an English cathedral into living history. We had arrived at a modern stone font close to the West door, and our guide pointed out that it had been carved as a memorial to George Bell, Bishop of Chichester from 1929–1958. Then, with great emphasis, he continued, "He was a *real* Christian."

We have chuckled many times since, because of our shared assumption that such a requirement was mandatory for episcopal consecration. But such was not necessarily the case during eras when ecclesiastical and political power were intertwined; and, as we know if we read history, being a *real* Christian often got bishops into trouble.

Richard, who turned his back on material security in order to pursue knowledge and risked the king's wrath because of his loyalty to Edmund, was a "real Christian." His prayer of gratitude to his "merciful redeemer, friend, and brother" reveals the source of his ability to follow his Lord, day by day, through all the reversals of his life.

Richard grew closer to that Lord through the activities we sing about in his hymn: "seeing," "loving," and "following." And Richard's prayer continues to provide a wise "three-step program" for Christians.

"To see thee more clearly." Our hymn uses the word "seeing" for "knowing." Seeing is a way of knowing, of gaining "insight" by looking. Faith, for Richard the scholar, begins with knowledge, and with gazing at the Lord in prayer. Richard's life's work began with "knowing" Jesus.

"Love thee more dearly." Our knowledge is not merely knowledge about, an accumulation of facts. It is knowledge of a Lord who bore pains and insults for humanity and bestowed upon us many benefits. Such knowledge leads inevitably to love. It may begin in the intellect, but it encompasses the heart as well.

"Follow thee more nearly." Love is not merely a "feeling," but an impetus for life and ministry. Richard's knowledge and love of Jesus as redeemer, friend, and brother was a catalyst. Richard's life followed the pattern of his Lord's, he also became friend and brother, expending the energy of love in service to others.

On the south wall of Chichester Cathedral are two Romanesque bas-reliefs from around 1125. Richard, once he was given permission by the king to function as bishop in his cathedral, would have passed these carvings often. On the left, Jesus is greeted at Bethany by a kneeling Mary and Martha; on the right, Jesus raises Lazarus from the tomb.

When I look at them, my gaze is always drawn to the face of Jesus. It is the face of compassion and love, the face, not of an aloof God, but of a merciful redeemer, friend, and brother. The face of one who walks beside us, as he walked beside Richard, day by day, day by day.

Proper 18: *The Sunday closest to September 7*

Hymn 606   Where true charity and love dwell
Latin; tr. Joyce MacDonald Glover (b. 1923)

The research into the origin of this text reads like a detective story. In 1924, the medievalist André Wilmart suggested that the hymn had originated, either at the beginning of the ninth century or in the first half of the eighth century, in a Benedictine monastery, where it was used for the weekly *mandatum* (foot washing) held on Saturday evenings.

In 1950, another scholar, Bernhard Bischoff, suggested that the hymn probably had been composed, not for the *mandatum* at the monastery, but for the *caritas* (in the Greek, *agapé*) meal on Maundy Thursday, and was eventually transferred to the foot washing during the tenth and eleventh centuries.

By 1954, Dag Norberg proposed a different origin, pointing out that the final stanza of the Latin hymn (not included in our English translation) was probably a prayer for the benevolence of the sovereigns Charlemagne and his son Pepin, King of Italy, under whose protection an ecclesiastical synod had assembled, presided over by Paulinus (ca. 750–802), Patriarch of Aquileia.

Paulinus was noted for his leading role in the discussions between the Byzantine Church and the West, and the synod may well have threatened to be a contentious one, since the debate centered around the controversial issue of whether to retain the usage of the *Filioque* clause (the words "and the Son") in the Creed. The Byzantine church, insisting that the

Holy Spirit proceeded only from the Father, wished to omit it, while the Western church, believing that the Spirit proceeded both from the Father and the Son, wished to retain the clause. (The synod eventually mandated the clause within the region.)

At the opening of the synod, Paulinus tried to set a moderating tone with an address based on Mt.18:20: "For where two or three are gathered in my name, there am I in the midst of them." Because this text is the underlying theme of *Ubi caritas*, and because Paulinus was also a writer of religious poetry, Norberg concluded that he was the likely author.

The translation of the Latin is by Joyce Glover, an adjunct professor of spirituality at Virginia Theological Seminary. It is a quite literal rendering of the Latin, retaining the rather unusual metre of the original.

The music, possibly even older than the text, may have originated within the Gallican rite: the liturgical tradition used in the churches of Gaul before Roman Gregorian chant was imposed by Pepin and Charlemagne.

ↄ

Modern life depends more and more on energy. Owing to its importance, new technologies which use energy sources like the wind and the sun are continually being developed. Because scientists warn that we are using up earth's resources of oil, gas, and coal at an alarming rate, we will be wise if we begin to depend, instead, on "sustainable energy," energy that will not be depleted by use.

The energy in food fuels our physical selves. The calories we consume are utilized in renewing our bodies and in providing us with strength as we go about our daily lives. If we miss too many meals, we are likely to feel weak and ill.

So far, we have found no "sustainable" food that will keep us going without eating.

There is another kind of energy, an energy that fuels our spirits and our interpersonal relationships. It is never depleted. Just the opposite: it increases as we use it.

The French scientist and theologian Teilhard de Chardin wrote of that energy: "The day will come when, after harnessing the ether, the winds, the tides and gravity, we shall harness for God the energies of love. And, on that day, for the second time in the history of the world, man will have discovered fire."[80]

Love is the ultimate sustainable energy, for its source is God. In fact, it is a sign of God's presence. "Where true charity and love dwell, God himself is there."

Fueling our lives with that energy, rather than with the energy of our petty jealousies and hatred, is like the difference between generating electricity from a solar panel that collects the rays of the sun, and generating it in an old-fashioned coal plant spewing forth black smoke. Love creates an atmosphere of unity rather than discord, of respect rather than enmity.

Loves takes many forms, but they flow from the same source. C.S.Lewis once wrote a book called *The Four Loves*, in which he analyzed love in terms of the categories of "Affection," "Friendship," "Eros," and "Charity." But if you have seen the play *Shadowlands*, about his marriage of convenience which grew from compassion to passion, you know that, in the end, Lewis would have found his love impossible to classify.

Whatever draws us from our preoccupation with self toward something beyond us is a sign of the love of God. Love transforms us, because it draws us to desire the well-being of something outside ourselves. Love, in all its forms, draws us to others, and it draws us to God. And when we gather with others in the name of Christ, love's energy increases exponentially: "For where two or three are gathered in my name, there am I in the midst of them." (Mt.18:20)

Where true charity and love dwell, God is there indeed.

Proper 19: *The Sunday closest to September 14*

Hymn 406, 407   Most High, omnipotent, good Lord
Francis of Assisi (1182–1226); tr. *Howard Chandler Robbins (1876–1952)*

Francis of Assisi is without doubt the most popular saint in Christian history. The son of a wealthy Italian cloth merchant, Francis spent his early youth in leading the young men of the city in their revels. In 1202, he served in a war between Assisi and Perugia and was held prisoner for a year. During this time, he began to reflect on the uselessness of his life. After his release, he began to have visions, and, when he visited the ruined chapel of St. Damiano outside Assisi, he heard a voice from the crucifix commanding him to "repair my house." He hurried home, gathered up most of the cloth in his father's warehouse, and rode off to Foligno, where he sold not only the cloth but also the horse. When his angry father brought him before the bishop, Frances stripped himself of his clothes, renounced both material possessions and family ties, and embraced a life of serving "Lady Poverty."

Soon others were inspired to join him, and he composed a simple rule of life which declared an aim "to follow the teachings of our Lord Jesus Christ and to walk in his footsteps." In 1210, the group went to Rome, and Pope Innocent III confirmed the Rule for the Order of Friars Minor. Over the following decade the brotherhood grew rapidly, and women under the leadership of a noblewoman named Clare formed a sister community. The Franciscans grew to number more than three thousand by the year 1221; the administration was more than Francis could handle, and he handed over the leadership.

His last years were spent in much suffering of body and spirit, but his joy never failed. He spent long periods of time in solitary prayer; during a forty day fast at the mountain retreat of La Verna, he received a vision of the crucified Christ, and, as the vision disappeared, he saw the wounds of Christ—the stigmata—on his own body. Francis survived another two years, almost blind and in great pain, cared for at the end by Clare and her nuns.

It was during this time that he composed "The Canticle of the Sun," the first great Italian poem in the vernacular, which was barely "out of its Latin swaddling clothes."[81] Its form was provided by the "Song of the Three Young Men," an apocryphal book which refers to the three pious Jews who were thrown into Nebuchadnezzar's furnace in the third chapter of Daniel. In his version, Francis names God's creatures as his brothers and sisters, and asks them to join him in this hymn of joy.

A month later, with war threatening to break out between Assisi and Perugia, Francis added a stanza to his canticle— "Be praised, my Lord, for those who pardon through your love. . . ." Francis's lines made such an impression that the factions forgave one another and war was prevented.

Finally, as Francis lay dying, he asked his brothers to sing

"The Canticle of the Sun," to which he added a final stanza welcoming "our sister, bodily death." Francis was proclaimed a saint a mere two years later.

The two tunes were composed for use with the text, the first for *The Hymnal 1940*, and the second for *The Hymnal 1982*.

౿

Francis is justly claimed as the patron saint of the environmental movement. The reason seems obvious; legends tell us that Francis preached to birds and tamed a wolf who was terrorizing the villagers of Gubbio. And, of course, we have this great canticle to demonstrate to us that Francis was in tune with nature. No wonder we place his statue beside the birdbath in the garden.

As we read Francis's story, however, we discover that Francis' connection with nature was no superficial thing. He enjoyed God's creation and sang the praises of the Creator. But his response did not stop with an aesthetic response to the world he saw around him. Like his contemporary, Richard of Chichester (see Hymn 654, Proper 17), "knowing" led to "loving" and thence to "following." Seeing the beauties of brother sun, sister moon, sister water, and mother earth led to caring, in the form of a universal love. That love led him into a different perception of his place in the world. Its outcome was Francis's simple yet radical Rule of absolute poverty, designed to guide himself and others in "following the teachings of our Lord Jesus Christ and to walk in his footsteps."

Early in life, he had depended for contentment on fine clothes, good food, and an assurance of a place in society. That contentment was replaced by the joy of knowing that he was, as a human being, part of the circle of all living creatures. Soon after his conversion, Francis kissed the hand of a leper—startling evidence of his sense of solidarity, not only with winged and four-legged creatures, but with the poorest of his fellow human beings. The perception that he was one with God's creation even made it possible, ultimately, for him to welcome death, nature's final cadence in the rhythm of earthly life.

One of the traits that has sometimes blocked the success of the environmental movement is that we stop at the first step. It is all too easy to rest content in an aesthetic enjoyment of the world around us.

Francis shows that we need also to connect with God's creation, to "kiss the leper" and "preach to the birds" by reaching out to the world around us, in whatever way we find ourselves called to do so. Francis would probably suggest that we can demonstrate our love of God's creation by such things as planting a tree, fighting urban sprawl, or helping schoolchildren create their own garden. It is more than likely he would point out that we should serve the lowliest in our society, not with arrogance, but as their brothers and sisters.

And he would point out that, before he himself set forth on his path, he stripped himself not only of his wealth but of his pride, standing naked before the bishop.

Francis asks us some hard questions. What wealth do those of us in the affluent "first world" need to share? Of what preconceptions, material possessions, or addictions, do we need to strip ourselves? We need to ponder our response to his challenge, with contrition and with prayer.

Proper 20: *The Sunday closest to September 21*

Hymn 9   Not here for high and holy things
Geoffrey Anketel Studdert-Kennedy (1833–1929)

Born in Leeds, Geoffrey Anketel Studdert-Kennedy was educated at Trinity College, Dublin University, and Ripon Theological College. He was ordained in the Church of England in 1908, and served as curate in Rugby and Leeds and then as vicar of St. Paul's, Worcester. As an army chaplain during World War I, he was known affectionately to thousands of soldiers as "Woodbine Willie" and was awarded the Military Cross. After the war, he was appointed chaplain to King George V and gained immense popularity in England and the United States as an original and eloquent preacher. From 1922 on, he was rector of St. Edmund's, Lombard Street, London.

A social activist, Studdert-Kennedy was a leader in the Industrial Christian Fellowship, and a prolific writer. This text appeared first in the author's collection *The Sorrows of God, and other poems* (London, 1921) under the title "At a Harvest Festival."

"Not here for high and holy things" evokes the displays of vegetables, fruit, grain, and flowers that decorate English parish churches at the annual festival marking the ingathering of the harvest. The text also has affinities with significant scriptural traditions, such as the psalmody praising the grandeur of God's creation (especially Psalms 8, 19, 33, 104, and 145).

Hymnologists Carl Daw and Robin Leaver describe the

opening stanzas as expressing "a romantic—even iconoclastic—piety that transfers to natural phenomena the conventional attributes of wealth and social status."[82] "Purple pageantry," "royal robes," "golden gates," "velvet," "silver glistering," are to be found, not in material wealth, but in the "common things of earth." It is an echo of Mt. 6:28–29 —"Consider the lilies of the field, how they grow; they neither toil nor spin, yet I tell you, even Solomon in all his glory was not clothed like one of these."

The tune, appropriate for a text which celebrates the English countryside, shares the melodic characteristics of many folksongs and ballads.

℘

A half century ago, the French scientist and theologian Pierre Teilhard de Chardin wrote:

> By means of all created things, without exception, the divine assails us, penetrates us and moulds us. We imagined it as distant and inaccessible, whereas in fact we live steeped in its burning layers. . . . As Jacob said, awakening from his dream, the world, this palpable world, to which we brought the boredom and callousness reserved for profane places, is in truth a holy place, and we did not know it.[83]

Some of the happiest people I know are those who realize that the common things of earth are holy, "charged with the grandeur of God"[84] As Teilhard said, "we live steeped in the burning layers" of the divine. The earth is but one of the veils through which we can glimpse the Lord of life.

In our time, humanity is becoming more and more disconnected from nature. For many of us, the greater part of our lives are spent indoors, often in artificial environments where even the "climate" is controlled. And as the pace of life becomes faster and faster, we have less and less time even to notice the common things of earth, let alone to include in our work the task of tending them. I think that part of the discontent of this generation has to do with our longing to re-connect with our earthly home—in the Greek, our *oikos*, which is the root of the word "ecology."

One of the remedies could be to include some time in our daily lives to contemplate the "common things of earth," which are so uncommonly complex and beautiful. This involves a change of awareness more than a change of schedule—from the "boredom and callousness" of which Teilhard wrote, to the awe which inspired "Not here for high and holy things."

As simple a thing as stepping outdoors—or looking out the window—can become an act of worship. Whether you live in the city or the country, the diamond dew of morning, the warmth of the giant noonday sun, and the velvet of night can awaken you to a whole "prayer book" written in the physical world. Just as praying the daily offices of Morning, Noonday, and Evening Prayer and Compline serve to remind us of God's presence in the words of Scripture and of our prayer tradition, so the moments we spend contemplating nature remind us of God's presence in every aspect of the physical world.

Such a change of attitude can transform some of our activities as well. The labor that brings us into direct contact with the things of the earth—from preparing food to shoveling snow or planting a garden—can become a sacrament, an outward and visible sign of our worship of the God whose holiness is embedded in all things.

No longer taking the world around us for granted will be like wakening from sleep. And our souls will be set ablaze, filled with new zest to serve the God who gave us such a sacred home.

Proper 21: *The Sunday closest to September 28*

Hymn 410   Praise, my soul, the King of heaven
Henry Francis Lyte (1793–1847)

Henry Francis Lyte was born in Scotland and received a Bachelor of Arts Degree from Trinity College, Dublin, where he received three poetry prizes. At first, he considered entering the medical profession, but he took holy orders in 1815. After being "jostled from one curacy to another," he became perpetual curate in 1823 of Lower Brixham, Devon, a fishing village, where he was to remain the rest of his life. He was never of robust health, and suffered from asthma and tuberculosis in his late years. Finding the labors of his parish to be undermining his strength, he went to the Continent to regain his health, but died in Nice at the age of fifty-four.

Three volumes of Lyte's poetry were published during his lifetime. "Praise, my soul, the King of heaven," a free paraphrase of Psalm 103, is taken from his collection, *The Spirit of the Psalms* (1834). The volume contained over two hundred eighty paraphrases, written for his congregation in Devon.

Erik Routley wrote: "Lyte was an obscure country curate who has no claim to fame beyond his saintly character and a handful of hymns."[85] In explaining why he wrote his hymns and poems, Lyte expressed himself in these words:

Might verse of mine inspire
One virtuous aim, one high resolve impart—
Light in one drooping soul a hallowed fire,
Or bind one broken heart,

Death would be sweeter then,
More calm my slumber 'neath the silent sod,
Might I thus live to bless my fellowmen,
Or glorify my God.[86]

The tune, composed especially for Lyte's text, is immensely popular and frequently sung at weddings.

☙

This hymn begins and ends with the picture of God as a king to whom we bring the tribute of our praises, singing—along with the sun, moon, and the angels—eternal "alleluias."

However, in the very center of this text, the image shifts. Instead of a glorious king, Lyte describes God as our infinitely understanding father who knows our "feeble frame": a father who tends, spares, and rescues us, gently bearing us in his hand.

One of my earliest memories is a visit to my grandparents' home in Minnesota. Beside their house was a cornfield, which seemed to me like a thousand-acre farm, but may have been only the neighbor's garden. One day, drawn by curiosity about what was in there, I wandered away from the safety of the back yard. I found out all too soon what was in there: corn, as far as I could see. Disoriented and frightened, because I could see only a patch of blue sky through the green stalks and golden tassels, I did the only thing I could do: I cried at the top of my lungs. Before long—although it seemed like an eternity—my father came, swept me up in his arms, and carried me to safety.

I have other memories of my father's carrying me. When we went to the beach in the summer, he would hoist me onto his shoulders and take me further and further into the crashing breakers. Exhilarated by the juxtaposition of the danger and absolute security, I would splash and play.

I do not remember much about the football games my parents took me to when they could not get a baby-sitter, but I do remember the crowds when the game was over. Sometimes I dared to walk down the stadium aisle myself in the dark shadows of all the tall people, tightly clasping an adult hand. But to be sure of making a safe exit, I much preferred being swung up on to my father's shoulders.

There has been much discussion in recent years about the exclusive use of male language in speaking of God. It is obvious that, since God is neither male nor female, we have, over the years, gotten things out of balance. My heart sings when I hear some of the maternal imagery in trial liturgies and new hymns.

I knew the love of a mother who cared passionately about her children, and I also have been in that role. Even so, I am sure our love did not begin to match God's maternal love. I would agree with the fourteenth-century Julian of Norwich, that "God rejoices that he is our mother."[87]

Because I was once a little girl who often had to be carried in the arms of her strong and protecting father, I'd hate to see us discard the notion that God can be like him, too.

Proper 22: *The Sunday closest to October 5*

Hymn 495   **Hail, thou once despisèd Jesus!**
John Bakewell (1721–1819) and *Martin Madan (1726–1790)*

Although this hymn was first issued anonymously in 1757, the author of the original is usually considered to be John Bakewell. Born in Derbyshire, Bakewell was converted about 1739 and began preaching as a Methodist evangelist in 1744. In London, he came to know the Wesley brothers, Martin Madan, Augustus Toplady, and other leaders of the evangelical movement. He was the author of religious verse, as well as a small number of hymns.

The expanded version of Bakewell's hymn was written by Martin Madan, a cousin of William Cowper. Like his cousin, Madan was called to the bar but never practiced as a barrister. Converted through a sermon of John Wesley, he was ordained in 1750 and became chaplain in the Lock Hospital, Hyde Park Corner, a charitable institution for women. A popular preacher and talented musician, he attracted other musical evangelicals; soon, the musical content of the services, together with regular performances of sacred oratorios, made Lock Hospital a fashionable place.

This hymn was published in the Lock Hospital Collection, *A Collection of Psalms and Hymns* (1760), which was printed for the worship of the chapel. Its companion book of tunes, published in 1769, became popularly known as "the Lock Hospital Collection." Both books became enormously influential on both sides of the Atlantic.

The hymn's early eighteenth-century Dutch melody,

evoking a solemn processional, is also used for Hymn 215 ("See the Conqueror mounts in triumph").

☙

This hymn takes sin seriously: "Thou didst suffer to release us . . . bearer of our sin and shame . . . all our sins on thee were laid . . . thou hast full atonement made." But it also raises some questions.

It is easy to misunderstand this kind of language. When we ponder the words of this hymn, it is all too tempting to think of the crucifixion as the result of a difference of opinion between the first and second Persons of the Trinity —a stern Father who is ready to punish humanity and a compassionate Son willing to sacrifice himself for us. But that surely cannot be. It is far from our understanding of the Trinity as a unity, bound together by love.

Instead, the crucifixion is a demonstration of the compassion of the Three in One, and One in Three—all together, like the medieval paintings of Jesus on Golgotha, with a bearded Father looking down from heaven and the Spirit hovering overhead. All three were suffering there, pouring out forgiveness on humankind.

The third stanza makes me ask a question: why, if we are truly reconciled with God, is it necessary for Jesus to keep reminding the Father to forgive us? Is it not, instead, the entire Trinity who keeps beckoning us back to goodness?

It is the forgiving love of God, in such contrast to our lack of that love, that should cause us to take sin seriously. But that doesn't mean we should wallow in guilt. In a memorable interview with Bill Moyers on public television, the inimitable Sister Wendy Beckett, art educator extraordinaire, proved also to be an astute theologian:

SISTER WENDY: . . . I don't think being truly human has any place for guilt.

BILL MOYERS: You don't?

SISTER WENDY: No. Contrition, yes. Guilt, no.

BILL MOYERS: And the difference is?

SISTER WENDY: Contrition means you tell God you are sorry and you're not going to do it again and you start off afresh. All the damage you've done to yourself, put right. Guilt means you go on and on belabouring and having emotions and beating your breast and being ego-fixated. Guilt is a trap. People love guilt because they feel if they suffer enough guilt, they'll make up for what they've done. Whereas, in fact, they're just sitting in a puddle and splashing. Contrition, you move forward.[88]

Sister Wendy would probably explain, if Bill Moyers had asked, that Jesus died on the cross to free us from the guilt that had trapped the human race into devising all kinds of sacrificial rituals to propitiate a judgmental and angry God. We don't have to do that any more. Instead, we can feel contrition, try to put things right, and—because Jesus' crucifixion showed us about God's love and forgiveness—move forward in freedom. No wonder we want to chant our Savior's praise!

Proper 23: *The Sunday closest to October 12*

Hymn 515   Holy Ghost, dispel our sadness
Paul Gerhardt (1607–1676); tr. *John Christian Jacobi (1670–1750) alt.*; *Augustus Montague Toplady (1740–1778)*

The origin of this hymn text is a ten-stanza prayer for Pentecost, *O du allersüsste Freude* ("O thou sweetest Source of Gladness"), written by Paul Gerhardt (see Hymn 168, Good Friday).

Gerhardt's poems represent the transition from an era when hymns were objective confessions of the faith to an era when hymns were of a more personal, devotional character. The change was brought about, in part, by the horrors of the Thirty Years War. People who had been surrounded by bloodshed and destruction sought comfort and consolation in a subjective and personal relationship with God. Robin Leaver writes that "In all this external devastation Gerhardt cultivated an inner spiritual strength that is evident in his poetry."[89]

The transition was to culminate in the Pietistic movement in the late seventeenth century and first half of the eighteenth century. A reaction against an orthodox formalism, it was to seek a restoration of the vigorous spiritual life Luther had preached, through an emphasis on Bible study, prayer, and works of Christian charity.

In 1725, John Christian Jacobi translated the hymn into English for his publication of *Psalmodia Germanica*. Jacobi, who was born in Thuringia, was a minor ecclesiastical figure at the English royal court. When George I came to the throne in 1714, Jacobi had come to England with other Hanoverian courtiers, and was appointed keeper of the Royal German Chapel at St. James' Palace.

The German hymns sung in the chapel caught the attention of the English public, and, to meet the demand, Jacobi translated fifteen of them and published them as *A Collection of Divine Hymns, Translated from the High Dutch* (1720). A second volume appeared in 1722, with a third, which contained this hymn, in 1725.

Several stanzas were rewritten by the fiery evangelical Augustus Toplady and circulated widely in the hymnals of evangelicals, both within and outside the Church of England, in the last quarter of the eighteenth century. The two stanzas in *The Hymnal 1982* consist of selected lines from the Jacobi-Toplady version.

The sturdy tune's minor mode changes halfway through to major, mirroring the passage from sadness to joy in the text.

℘

I have been in several parishes that were grieving.

When I was in high school, two respected and greatly loved priests in my parish church suddenly announced that they were leaving the Episcopal Church to become Roman Catholics. It turned our world upside down to think that the men who had taught us about our branch of the faith had turned their backs on it, and there were many years of sadness and confusion.

The church in my college town went through a schism. Parishioners formed two congregations—one of them met in the church, and one in the college chapel—and people on opposing sides of the conflict tried to avoid one another—a difficult feat in a small town. Although united once again, parishioners still speak of those days with obvious pain.

A rector in a nearby town clashed with his vestry. Differences of opinion led to acrimonious meetings and finally to his resignation. He left, along with several pillars of the parish. The parish took a long time to get over a communal depression and sense of loss.

I think that if I were the rector or organist of a church dealing with the grief of a parish community, I would ask that Gerhardt's hymn be sung every Sunday. It tells us what to do when sadness so infuses our lives that it seems as if we will never be happy again. "Holy Ghost, dispel our sadness . . . come, thou source of joy and gladness, breathe thy life, and spread thy light."

What we would pray for is a new Pentecost, bringing the peaceful Spirit of Christ to dwell in each aching, angry, or disillusioned heart. We would ask for the Spirit to heal our wounded pride and our broken hope. We would ask the Spirit to empower us to persevere, trusting that God can do greater things than we can imagine.

All three churches I mentioned emerged from their difficult times with new dedication to the mission and ministry of Jesus Christ. But the healing of a community is a gradual process, like the healing of a physical wound. Slowly but surely the Spirit worked among them, turning turbulence into peace, and disorientation into new motivation to do the work of God.

The pattern of the Spirit's work in the world was clearly visible. It is the work of resurrection, the work of bringing things to life again.

When we pray that the Spirit come among us, we should not be surprised that resurrection happens to us as well, and that we become, through the power of God, a new creation.

Proper 24: *The Sunday closest to October 19*

Hymn 683, 684   O for a closer walk with God
William Cowper (1731–1800)

During Cowper's residence at Olney (See Hymn 677, Proper 12), he stayed with a Mrs. Mary Unwin, who remained his devoted friend and guardian till the end of her days. (The house is now a museum containing relics, books, and portraits of Cowper and his friends.) Behind the home is a garden where Cowper and the parish priest John Newton met nearly every day to work on their hymns. "O for a closer walk" is said to have been written on December 9, 1769, when Mrs. Unwin was gravely ill. In a letter written to his aunt the following day, Cowper wrote:

> She is the chief of blessings I have met with in my journey since the Lord was pleased to call me. . . . Her illness has been a sharp trial to me. Oh, that it may have a sanctified effect, that I may rejoice to surrender up to the Lord my dearest comforts, the moment He may require them. . . . I began to compose the verses yesterday morning before daybreak, but fell asleep at the end of the first two lines [stanzas?]: when I awaked again, the third and fourth were whispered to my heart in a way I have often experienced.[90]

Mrs. Unwin was to recover, but she would suffer a series of paralytic strokes beginning in 1791. In 1793, Cowper would write the beautiful poem "To Mary."

Cowper's poems are plaintive, tender, and refined, and

are largely transcripts of his own immediate feelings. Although he wrote much fine devotional material, he was continually troubled by doubts about his own salvation. (*The Oxford Companion to English Literature* comments, "Whether religion was the cause or cure of his depression has been much disputed.")[91]

Elizabeth Barrett Browning paid Cowper this tribute:

O Christians, at your cross of hope a hopeless hand
    was clinging:
O men, this man in brotherhood your weary paths
    beguiling,
Groaned inly while he taught you peace, and died
    while ye were smiling!
And now, what time you all may read through dim-
    ming tears his history,
How discord on the music fell and darkness on the
    glory, and
How when, one by one, sweet sounds and wandering
    lights departed,
He wore no less a loving face because so broken-
    hearted.[92]

The first musical setting of the hymn is a Victorian tune; the second, a Scottish psalm tune.

❧

"Where is the blessedness I knew when first I saw the Lord?" Many people ask that question, although most of us do not suffer the kind of torment that the poet Cowper knew. Why does it sometimes feel as if God is absent? Has God actually left us, because of something we have done? Or do we have unreal expectations of what religious experience should be?

Is God with us, even at the those times when we do not experience the divine presence?

At some point in their lives, some people have experienced a "closer walk with God" through moments when they had a special sense that the Creator dwelt within them, or that Jesus was beside them, or that the Spirit called them to ministry. They may have felt God almost palpably; they were exhilarated and energized. It was like a glass of heady wine. It was like falling in love.

Cowper thought that the reason his "closer walk with God" did not continue was his fault—because of his sins which drove God away, or of his "idols" which took God's place. He thought that God had withdrawn.

It is true that sometimes we ourselves erect the barricades that hamper our walks with God, but God does not ever do so. God will never be "driven away"; rather, God eternally pursues us with love. In Cowper's case, it was probably the extreme fatigue and anxiety about Mrs. Unwin's illness, along with his innate melancholia, that made it seem as if God were absent.

Usually, however, the reason our sense of "blessedness" changes is that change is built into the universe, including human relationships and our relationship with the divine.

The assumption that emotional peaks will continue unaltered leads to disappointment and frustration. Our expectations can sour the growth toward a mature love that is much richer than the elation we first felt. In the domain of human relationships, those who have known long marriages know that the thrills of romance are just the beginning of love. Romance blossoms into something much better.

The poet Amy Lowell compares first love and mature love to the difference between wine and bread:

When you came, you were like red wine and honey,
And the taste of you burnt my mouth with its
    sweetness.
Now you are like morning bread,
Smooth and pleasant.
I hardly taste you at all for I know your savour,
But I am completely nourished.[93]

Similarly, our first inebriation with God fills us with "spirit," so that we can know God also in the "breadness," the ordinariness of life.

Perhaps God seduces us through occasional glimpses of blessedness, so that we will become faithful partners in our ordinary lives. Being married involves living with the beloved in all circumstances, morning, noon, and night. Perhaps God serves us the heady wine of religious experience from time to time to encourage us to partake of the bread of faithful companionship that is the closest of all walks with God.

Proper 25: The Sunday closest to October 26

Hymn 610   Lord, whose love through humble service
Albert F. Bayly (1901–1984)

Albert F. Bayly was born at Bexhill-on-Sea in Sussex. He served as a shipwright in the Royal Dockyard School in Portsmouth, but in 1925 decided to study at Mansfield College in Oxford and become a Congregational minister. He began to write hymns in 1945 and went on to publish five collections of them. He served many Congregational churches in England until his retirement in 1972. Bayly was an honorary fellow of Westminster Choir College, Princeton, New Jersey, an honorary vice-president of the Hymn Society, and was honored at a special service in Westminster Abbey in 1978. He died in Chichester in 1984.

Bayly wrote this hymn in response to a joint appeal by the Hymn Society of America and the Department of Social Welfare of the National Council of Churches of Christ in the United States for hymns which would "express the interrelationship of worship and service of love as expressions of one deep, abiding faith in God."[94] It was included in the booklet *Seven New Social Welfare Hymns* (1961) and chosen as the Conference Hymn for the Second National Conference of Churches and Social Welfare in Cleveland, Ohio in October of that year.

The text, rich in scriptural references, relates the mission of Jesus to the lives of contemporary Christians. The poet's wide acquaintance with classic hymnody is revealed in the fourth stanza, where he uses the phrase "Forth in thy dear name we go," which echoes Charles Wesley's opening line "Forth in thy Name, O Lord, I go."

Bayly's text is matched with a Welsh hymn tune.

∽

All during the year, solicitations for money from worthy organizations pour into our mailbox. I open the mail at our kitchen table and read about the urgent need for money to feed indigent children in Africa or the homeless in New York City, to save the rain forests in South America or the old growth in the Northwest, to support a great art museum or a local choral society.

Sometimes I am asked to donate my time and energy instead of my money. I am given opportunities to landscape a bike trail, to work for voter registration, to build a Habitat for Humanity house, to join a citizen's committee on urban sprawl, or to drive for Meals on Wheels. If ever I wished I had unlimited resources of time, energy and money, it is when I sit before the pile of mail on our kitchen table.

When we take seriously God's call to love our neighbors as ourselves through compassionate action, we can become overwhelmed. That is when I need the prayer: "As we worship, grant us vision . . . making known the needs and burdens your compassion bids us bear." To make the prayer clearer, I might substitute "making known *which* needs and burdens your compassion bids us bear."

Because we can't each do everything. God doesn't expect each of us to "save the world" alone.

But how do we discover which needs we are each meant to address? How do we discover which burdens God calls us to bear?

The great Trappist monk and writer, Thomas Merton, once advised, "Mind your own business." In our lives, he suggested, we each have our own "business" given us by God, a path uniquely our own.

When we think about the business of ministry, "our business" is whatever need in the world particularly "calls to us" as we pray—or as we open that pile of mail or take special notice of needs that are closest to us. While my mother-in-law's sight was failing, for example, my husband took special pleasure in supporting organizations that served the blind.

"Our business" makes use of our gifts to help to heal the world's wounds, rather than those gifts which we do not have. In our ministry, we may be called to forth in God's dear name "to the child, the youth, the aged." Notice that there are commas between those words, which we might even replace with the word "or"! The same people who thrive on working with young children or with the youth group may not necessarily be those with pastoral skills in a nursing home.

If our ministry is truly "our business," it brings us satisfaction and, even, pleasure, no matter how difficult it may be. Is our ministry in the world a good match for our personality? Do we like to attend meetings and to work through the political process, or do we find such activities frustrating and upsetting? Do we thrive in a group setting, or do we feel more ourselves when we work one-on-one? Do we like to teach, or do we prefer rolling up our sleeves and working with our hands?

When we respond to God's love by giving ourselves and our gifts in this way, we will be both "minding our own business" and doing the greater business of providing hope and health, good will and comfort, to a world in deep need of the love of God.

All Saints' Day: November 1

Hymn 287   For all the saints, who from their labors rest
William Walsham How (1823–1897)

William Walsham How wrote the text of "For all the saints" in 1864, for use on All Saints Day. It was originally entitled "Saints Day Hymn—Cloud of Witnesses—Heb. 12:1" and intended as a commentary on "I believe in the communion of saints."

William How was an Anglican clergyman who ministered in several cures in rural England, became chaplain of the English Church in Rome, Suffragan Bishop of East London, and the first Bishop of Wakefield, and was particularly known for his work on behalf of the poor in the east end of London. Affectionately known as "the poor man's bishop," he is reported to have declined the bishopric of Manchester without even bothering to tell his family, and later refused the same post at Durham, a position that would have doubled his salary.

He once wrote a description of the ideal minister of the Gospel: "Such a minister should be a man pure, holy, and spotless in his life; a man of much prayer; in character meek, lowly, and infinitely compassionate; of tenderest love to all; full of sympathy for every pain and sorrow, and devoting his days and nights to lightening the burdens of humanity."[95] People who knew him said it was almost a perfect description of How himself, who had engraved on his pastoral staff the saying of St. Bernard: *Pasce verbo, pasce vita* ("Feed with the Word; feed with the life.")

He was also a champion of ecumenism and of liberal theology within the Anglican Church. Attempting to reconcile science and the Bible, he wrote, "Evolution is the wonderful way in which the Lord formed man out of the dust of the ground."

How received honorary doctorates from the Archbishop of Canterbury in 1879 and from Oxford in 1886. He died while vacationing in Ireland, and was greatly mourned by those he directly served, as well as by the Christian church at large, for he had become known for his writings, which included about fifty-four hymns. His hymns embody an ideal he once expressed: "A good hymn should be like a good prayer—simple, real, earnest, and reverent."[96]

Ralph Vaughn Williams wrote the tune expressly for

How's text in 1906. At first it was criticized by some as being "jazz music"; now it is considered to be one of the finest hymn-tunes written during the twentieth century.

ↁ

I have sung this hymn every All Saints' Day, remembering the great saints of the church who are part of the "great company of heaven." Just as I remember my friends, family, and mentors with gratitude and affection on their birthdays, so on this day I think of my favorite saints. We all probably have our favorites—saints who have stepped off their pedestals or out of their stained glass windows—and come to life for us.

On All Saints' Day, I celebrate some of these companions who have guided me over the years with their insights. The saints of the early church have left their legacy in the Gospels, the Epistles, and the stories of the martyrs. But I also think of some soul-sisters who lived after Biblical times: the visionary Hildegard of Bingen, a renaissance woman long before the Renaissance; Julian of Norwich, who saw a loving God in all that exists; the irrepressible Teresa of Avila, reformer and mystic. I think of my brothers in Christ: Francis of Assisi, who sang a canticle of Creation both with his poem and with his life; and John of the Cross, who sought Love in the soul's dark night.

I think of those who have not been awarded official sainthood, but are also God's blessed ones. I think of George Herbert in the seventeenth century, the faithful pastor and poet. I remember Evelyn Underhill, the scholarly and quiet teacher of prayer.

I think also of Desmond Tutu, whom I met when he visited Trinity Church, Wall Street. A small man, he became ten feet tall when he preached. Although I knew he was a man of courage and often risked his physical safety for the cause of justice, the most remarkable thing about him was his ebullience, and a smile that lit up the world around him. Desmond Tutu was totally there. Once, when I asked him to sign one of his books for me before a service, he wrote with such attention to what he was doing that he didn't notice that the entire procession was waiting for him to finish.

Elaine Ramshaw writes:

> One of the tasks of the church, in its liturgical life as well as in its formal education, is to recall the history of humanity in a different way than is usual in secular society. The church . . . remembers a different sort of hero. . . . Rather than see such people as human-interest sidebar stories in a history focused on the wielders of power, the liturgical calendar puts them in center stage of the history that matters.[97]

I am glad that we recognize that the saints—both the Saints we honor in our Church Year and the saints who cross our paths—should be in center stage. Perhaps that is the reason this hymn is frequently used at funerals. Its images of endurance and victory seem especially appropriate for those faithful Christians whose final years have, because of illness or extreme old age, been a struggle. They, also, deserve a song of praise, and a final "Alleluia!"

Proper 26: *The Sunday closest to November 2*

Hymn 665   All my hope on God is founded

Robert Seymour Bridges (1844–1930), alt., after Joachim Neander (1650–1680)

Joachim Neander was the foremost hymn writer of the German Reformed Church, the "Paul Gerhardt of the Calvinists." After a boisterous student life typical of seventeenth-century Germany, Neander served as a tutor in Frankfort and Heidelberg. He was introduced to Pietism (see Proper 23, Hymn 515), and became acquainted with the movement's leader, Philip Spener. Neander became headmaster of the grammar school at Düsseldorf, and five years later went to serve as an unordained assistant in a church in Bremen. However, because of his zealous religious practices and preaching, he was frequently in trouble with the church authorities. He sought release in communion with nature, in prayer, and in composing hymns. His great love of nature often led him to the valley of Düssel, ultimately named after him as the "Neanderthal" (Neander Valley), where it is said that he wrote many of his hymns. (It was here in 1856 that the skeleton of *Homo neanderthalensis* was discovered.) Neander died of tuberculosis at the age of thirty, having already produced sixty hymns.

Robert Bridges, the son of a wealthy squire, was educated at Eton and Corpus Christi College, Oxford, after which he studied medicine at St. Bartholomew's Hospital. His plan was to practice medicine until the age of forty and then devote himself to poetry, but he had to give up his practice because of ill health a few years before his planned retirement. He then moved to the Berkshire village of Yattendon where he lived and wrote for the next thirty years. A prolific writer, he was a friend of Gerard Manley Hopkins, whose complete poems Bridges eventually published.

His work with the village choir led him to an interest in hymnody and to the publication of the landmark collection, the *Yattendon Hymnal*, considered "easily the most distinguished of individual contributions to modern hymnology." Forty-four of the hymns in the *Yattendon Hymnal* were translations or adaptations by Bridges himself. Erik Routley writes that Bridges "did more than any other person to raise English hymnody to the level of respectable literature, redeeming it from both the crudity of the 18th c. and the conventionality of the 19th."

Bridges was named poet laureate in 1913; he continued writing until 1929, when his magnum opus, the *Testament of Beauty*, was published.

"All my hope on God is founded" was said by Bridges to be "a free version of a hymn by Joachim Neander." He did not really translate his German originals, but used them merely as a suggestion, sometimes adding new verses of his own. Percy Dearmer pointed out that, "although the individualistic note of the post-Luther German pietism is here retained in the opening stanzas, the hymn is on the whole on a wider and more modern note, and in line with [Bridge's] final mature thought in the *Testament of Beauty*."[98]

The tune was written by the composer Herbert Howells, who recalled that, upon receiving a request for a hymn tune, he wrote it in its entirety while still at the breakfast table where he had been opening the mail. The tune honors the composer's son Michael, who died in childhood.

☙

"All my hope on God is founded." But how do we know we can depend on that hope? Does God truly wish to shower us with blessings? This hymn suggests a joyous answer: that one of the ways we know we can depend on God is through the beauty that surrounds us.

I suspect that the reason Joachim Neander found the solace of God during his walks in the verdant valley of Düssel, and Robert Bridges found comfort during an illness which cut short the course of his medical career, was their jubilant certainty that God desired them to share their Creator's joy. Bridges was later to write of "Beauty, the eternal Spouse of the Wisdom of God and Angel of his Presence thru' all creation, fashioning her new love-realm in the mind of man."[99]

Beauty is one of God's "lures" in winning us over: "pleasure leads us where we go." I remember a self-proclaimed atheist who finally made his way into my meditation class at Trinity Church after months of attending the weekday concert series. As he listened to great music in that holy space, he had begun to consider, for the first time, that there might be a reality behind the events of everyday life. He now calls himself an agnostic, and God is not done with him yet. He continues to explore the mystery behind music's power to move and enchant him.

Even the very young can perceive the sacred through their encounters with beauty. In a pre-school class in which I used the arts in Christian education, I brought in a collection of old Christmas cards which depicted the Annunciation of the Angel Gabriel to Mary, and let the children pick their favorites. One energetic little boy zeroed in on a Renaissance painting, his eyes alight—"I've got to have this!" —and clasped it to his heart.

For people like this little boy, God shines through such a painting; for others, music is God's voice. For others, it is poetry, or dance, or the loveliness of nature. It is the jubilation of our souls in response to these things that causes them to be channels of the divine. And when they become such channels, they convey the mystery of the Creator, the love of the Son, and the energy of the Spirit, better than any theological treatise.

When we are in despair, we ache for God's solace. But God calls to us also through our moments of pure delight. They reassure us that we can found our hope on a God who loves us.

The gift of beauty is a healing gift; through it, God's creativity constantly strengthens and renews us as human beings. In fashioning things of beauty ourselves, we share something of what it means to be made in the image of God.

As beings made in God's image, we become more fully human when we allow ourselves to find pleasure in the exquisiteness with which God has surrounded us. After all, God's greatest gift, Jesus Christ, was not only Goodness, Wisdom, and Truth personified: he was also a human being, able to take pleasure in good wine at a wedding feast. God wants us to enjoy the bounteous gifts we are daily given. And that is a God on whom I am willing to found all my hope!

Proper 27: The Sunday closest to November 9

Hymn 620   Jerusalem, my happy home
F. B. P. (ca. 16th cent.)

The earliest manuscript of this hymn is in the British Museum. Although the manuscript has been dated about 1616, the hymn is thought to be older. Entitled, "A Song Made by F. B. P. To the tune of Diana," the original has twenty-six stanzas. A similar hymn exists from 1585, by W. Prid, "O mother dear, Jerusalem," of forty-four stanzas, which suggests that both must have had an earlier common source.

That source seems to be a passage in the popular *Liber Meditationum*, at one time falsely attributed to St. Augustine. This widely popular book was translated by both Roman Catholics and Protestants at the time of the Reformation.

"Jerusalem, my happy home" and "O mother dear, Jerusalem" were copied extensively by seventeenth-century hymn writers. These later versions often appeared as broadsides (a large sheet of paper printed on one side) because this was an inexpensive and convenient way to distribute them at a time when hymns were beginning to become popular in England.

The writer, "F. B. P." was probably a Roman Catholic, and possibly a priest. There have been surmises that he was Francis Baker, Pater (or priest), who in 1593 was imprisoned in the Tower of London.

Lionel Adey points out that, if Baker was indeed the author, it is not surprising that he explored every image of heaven except those of palace and court! Within the original twenty-six stanzas, "F. B. P." imagines, in Adey's words, a "happy harbour of saints, a city with gates of pearl and golden streets, a paradise of 'vineyards and orchards' and, chiefly, the Church Triumphant wherein 'our Lady sings Magnificat,' SS. Ambrose and Augustine the 'Te Deum.' For the most part, however, his poem consists of negations. Saints know not sorrow, toil, sickness, or the fear of death. Jerusalem knows no mist of terror or darkness of confinement, for 'God himself gives light.' The poet views heaven and the life he knows as mutually exclusive."[100]

The five stanzas chosen for *The Hymnal 1982* are set to an American folk tune, very suitable to the naive charm of the poem.

෴

Very recently, I went to visit Ed, a ninety-seven-year old acquaintance, in a nursing home. I had received a telephone call that Ed, who had not been doing well was probably going to die that day, and that a priest's visit would help him through the process of letting go. Ed was anxious and fearful when I arrived, but, after the hospice nurse and I had said the prayers for the dying and anointed him, he quieted down, and said, "I'm peaceful now. I want to go home."

Those who spend time with the dying, especially the elderly, know that it is not unusual for a dying person to say, "I want to go home." We know very well that "home" does not refer to any dwelling-place on this earth. It means the dwelling-place of God.

It is impossible to know what that dwelling-place is like, but, over the centuries people have tried to imagine it. Some of them, like our hymnwriter, paint pictures of heaven that have the naiveté and charm of a child's drawing. The twenty-six stanzas of the original poem show us a city built of precious stones, gold, and ivory. In its green gardens even cinnamon and sugar grow—no need to ply the trade routes any longer—and abundant orchards provide rare fruit. There is no sickness, no "dampish mist," no envy, nor hunger, but only pleasure. There the saints dwell: David, with harp in hand, Our Lady Mary, and (in the original) Saints Ambrose, Augustine, and Magdalene.

There are more sophisticated pictures of heaven, like that of the Italian poet Dante Alighieri, who described in his *Paradiso* his journey through a realm of planets inhabited by various saints, as he moves ever closer to God, the reality at the heart of heaven. He finally sees that reality in the vision of an immense white rose, formed of a myriad of saints, each one distinct. He fixes his gaze on the center of the rose, and finally sees three spheres, each distinct yet occupying one space. As he gazes at this image of the Trinity, he sees the vision of Christ, and finds himself wholly in tune with "the love that moves the sun and the other stars."

These two pictures, as different as they are, have a common denominator. They are each the picture of what the poet—either "F. B. P." or Dante Alighieri—most desires. F. B. P., probably in disgrace with the court and confined in a "dampish" cell in the grey tower beside the Thames, hopes that, after death, he will live in a beautiful and rich city, along with the spiritual companions he knows from Scripture. The poet Dante, on the other hand, wants a mystical vision, and finally attains it after conversing with a whole roll call of the saints of his time as well as of the past.

That's the best we can do: imagine that heaven is exactly what we most desire. I still shudder when I think of a first-grade Sunday School classmate, whose dog had just died, asking the teacher if he would see his dog in heaven. The teacher drew herself up and, with great authority, answered, "No. You can't have your dog in heaven, but God will give you another dog, if you still want one there."

Even in first grade, I knew that wasn't true. In fact, I knew it was ridiculous. If heaven is endless joy, we will have —in some sense—our bejeweled cities and pet dogs. When we finally stand close to God's burning love, we are likely to discover that God contains all that was and is and ever shall be, including our humblest desires.

Proper 28: The Sunday closest to November 16

Hymn 680   O God, our help in ages past
Isaac Watts (1674–1748)

Isaac Watts (see Hymn 100, Christmas Day) is often called the father of English hymnody. He displayed the symptoms of his vocation at a very early age. The story goes that he had an annoying habit of rhyming even everyday conversation; one day, when he was scolded by his irritated father for this practice, he cried out, "O, Father, do some pity take, and I will no more verses make."

Despite poor health, he was to become a scholar in many different fields. His works, among which were essays, discussions of psychology, sermons, catechisms, theological treatises, and textbooks on logic, wielded a powerful influence upon the thinking of the late seventeenth and early eighteenth centuries. His poetic gifts were such as to prompt Samuel Johnson to include Watts in his *Lives of the Poets*. His lasting fame, however, eventually rested on his hymns and paraphrases. When he died, a monument honoring him was placed in Westminster Abbey.

"O God, our help in ages past," a paraphrase of Psalm 90, can be found in practically every English language hymnal in the world. It was written around the year 1714, when Queen Anne was near death and there was widespread anxiety about her successor. Many people feared that England would soon be torn by civil strife.

The hymn, originally containing nine stanzas, was published in Watts' *The Psalms of David* in 1719.

It is considered to be one of finest texts in English hymn literature, and was sung at Sir Winston Churchill's funeral on January 30, 1965, in St. Paul's Cathedral, London.

Handel used the tune, by William Croft, in an anthem entitled "O Praise the Lord" and Bach used it in his great Fugue in E-flat Major, often called the "St. Anne Fugue"; its matching with Watts' text did not occur until early in the nineteenth century.

❧

Our era is an exciting one. We are on the move! We are able to see more of the world than at any time in history. Modern transportation can whisk us across an ocean or a continent in a few hours. We can choose to leave one job in order to work in a more challenging or more lucrative one many miles away. We put our home on the market, and go house-hunting in a distant city. People seldom spend all their lives in one place.

I did !ive in one place for my first twenty-three years, with the exception of my years at college. As a child, I was so fond of my home that I couldn't imagine ever moving. I remember weeping when, one night after I had been tucked into bed, I overheard my parents discuss "moving to

Connecticut." (We didn't.) When I was in third grade and went away with a classmate for a week at her family's beach cottage, the ache to return home finally became so acute that, by the time I was deposited at my door, I had dissolved into tears. After my father died and my mother decided to move to an apartment, I could not believe she was selling my childhood home, although by that time my husband and I had our own. History repeated itself many years later, when we decided to sell our children's childhood home, and the youngest, who had returned to the nest after graduate school, felt similarly uprooted. As I remember, he said, "You could at least wait until I could afford to buy it."

Whether we live for many years in one place, or lead a more transient life-style, a home remains both a necessity and a symbol. Our home is our shelter, our protection, a place of comfort where we can be ourselves. It is painful when our homes are places of discord or abuse, and it is even more of a tragedy should we be one of the too many men, women, and children who have no home at all.

For along with the thirst for change and new experiences lies a universal hunger for stability. And that is probably the reason most of us love our homes.

Our homes may be symbols of that stability, but they do not suffice in the long run. They themselves are transitory, subject to the whims of weather and aging. Their roofs and walls may have sheltered the lives of our families, but they are no more permanent than our own bodies. I hear the reminder in the haunting "Here on earth have we no continuing place" in the Brahms *Requiem*, and I read the reminder in the news and the obituaries of every newspaper I open.

Earthly life is impermanent. If we depend on it for stability, we will be spiritually homeless.

Where is stability? "Lord, you have been our refuge, from one generation to another. Before the mountains were brought forth, or the land and the earth were born, from age to age you are God." Our stability, "while life shall last" and also beyond death, is God, our eternal home.

Proper 29: *The Sunday closest to November 23*

Hymn 450, 451   All hail the power of Jesus' name!
Edward Perronet (1726–1792)

Edward Perronet was born into a family of Huguenot refugees who went to England from Switzerland in 1680 and became members of the Church of England. His father was vicar of Shorehand, Kent, for fifty years and enjoyed the friendship and esteem of Charles and John Wesley. Perronet himself originally intended to take Anglican orders, but he became deeply involved with the Wesleys and chose the life of an itinerant Methodist preacher. A man of independent mind and volatile temper, he eventually led the secession of the Methodists from the Church of England, against the wishes of the Wesleys.

He became connected with several dissenting religious groups and was appointed one of the of Countess of Huntingdon's ministers in a chapel in Watling Street, Cambridge. After he had displeased her also, he spent the remainder of his days in a small Independent chapel in Canterbury.

The story is told that one day, when he was still in John Wesley's good graces, Wesley spotted him in his congregation and announced that Perronet would preach at the service the following morning. Perronet felt he could not properly decline, yet he did not want to preach in presence of the great evangelist. His solution was to announce, "I am compelled by the respect I have for Mr. Wesley to occupy his place. I am entirely inadequate to the task; but, for all that, I will give you the best sermon that has ever been delivered." He then read the Sermon on the Mount in its entirety without comment and concluded the service.

Perronet (probably fortunately) is remembered today chiefly because he wrote this hymn, which appeared first in John Rippon's *A Selection of Hymns, from the Best Authors intended to be an Appendix to Dr. Watt's Psalms and Hymns.* Perronet titled each stanza: "Angels," "Martyrs," "Converted Jews," "Believing Gentiles," "Sinners of Every Age," "Sinners of Every Nation," and "Ourselves." (The last has been omitted in *The Hymnal 1982.*)

The eighteenth-century tune has, from the beginning, been matched to Perronet's text.

℘

The spirit of "All hail the power of Jesus' Name!" makes me think of the the Fourth of July parades the children in our neighborhood would put together each year in the years immediately following World War II. We would march around and around the block with toy drums and anything else that made noise, waving small flags and singing "Hooray for the red, white, and blue." In our unalloyed patriotism, it never occurred to us that our country could be wrong about anything. In school assemblies, we loved to face the flag, in its brass stand on the left side of the gymnasium stage, say the Pledge of Allegiance with our hands over our hearts, and then belt out "Oh say, can you see" at the tops of our lungs.

Many years later, when our country was mired in Vietnam, I did not want to even look at an American flag. The flag which was once placed in a bracket at the peak of our front porch roof was taken down, and rested furled in our coat closet. I thought often during that time about how out of step I felt with the leadership of this country. There was no way I would have joined a parade—unless it were a peace march.

Most people who have lived long enough have felt similar ambivalence about the policies of their native lands. Disillusionment may be caused by many issues. Charismatic leaders turn out to be all too human; princes and princesses separate and divorce.

Or perhaps there is a shattering of your trust in someone's leadership, not in the national arena, but in your personal or professional life. Perhaps, if you are Edward Perronet, you part ways with the revered Wesleys—no matter that it was probably your fault.

The great Indian prophet Mohandas Ghandi once said that there were only two successful ways to deal with worldly power. One was to have all the power. The other was to have none. Ghandi, once a student of Christianity (he said he thought it was a wonderful religion—it was just a pity people didn't practice it) chose the latter.

Inevitably, we will discover flaws in our human leaders, whether they be presidents or princes or priests. No amount of patriotism or politicking can cause it to be otherwise. We may wish with all our hearts that we can put our fate in the hands of our leaders, but we cannot. Power in the hands of human beings is always flawed by our lack of wisdom, our character traits, our timidity, and our ego-centricity. We must never be blind followers; we must modify the power of our leaders by empowering ourselves and our communities, as well.

There is only one leader whom we can safely trust: Christ our King. He is a strange kind of king: a king who was powerless politically, an itinerant preacher and healer who was crowned with thorns and put to death as a criminal. Because his reign is based on love, he in fact, has more power—and that, uncorrupted—than any earthly leader has ever glimpsed. In him, we dare to put our trust, and to sing, without any qualifying adverbs, "Crown him Lord of all!"

Thanksgiving Day

Hymn 396, 397   Now thank we all our God
Martin Rinckart (1586–1649); tr. *Catherine Winkworth (1827–1878)*

Martin Rinckart was born in Eilenburg, Saxony, and for a time was a boy chorister in the famous St. Thomas Church of Leipzig, where J. S. Bach was later to be musical director. He worked his way through the University of Leipzig and was ordained to the ministry of the Lutheran Church. At the age of thirty-one, he was called to be the pastor in his native town.

Rinckart arrived just when the bloodshed of the Thirty Years War was beginning. Because it was a walled city, Eilenburg became an overcrowded refuge for political and military fugitives, and the Rinckart home served as a refuge, although Rinckart often had difficulty in providing food and clothing for his own family. Waves of deadly pestilence and famine swept the city, and during the great plague of 1637, the city's officials and clergy either died or ran away, leaving Rinckart alone to care for the dead. He read the burial service forty to fifty times each day, including a service for his own wife. By the end of the war, eight thousand people had died in Eilenburg, and the burials finally had to be in trenches, without a service.

During the closing years of the war Eilenberg was overrun in turn by both the Austrian and the Swedish armies. During one of the occupations by the Swedes, a large tribute payment was demanded of the city's already impoverished citizens. Rinckart attempted to intercede with the army's leaders. The story is told that, when the commander would not consider his request, Rinckhart turned to his parishioners and said, "Come, my children, we can find no mercy with man; let us take refuge with God," and they all fell to their knees in prayer and sang a familiar hymn. The Swedish commander was so moved that he lowered the levy.

Amazingly, in the midst of this turmoil, Rinckart managed to produce seven dramas about the events of the Reformation, as well as a total of sixty-six hymns.

"Now thank we all our God" originated as a family tablegrace for Rinckart's children to sing. It is based on Sir. 50:22–24:

> And now bless the God of all, who everywhere works great wonders, who fosters our growth from birth, and deals with us according to his mercy.
>
> May he give us gladness of heart, and may there be peace in our days in Israel, as in the days of old.
>
> May he entrust to us his mercy, and may he deliver us in our days!

The hymn was sung to celebrate the Peace of Westphalia, December 10, 1648, that ended the Thirty Years War.

This "German Te Deum" transcends all national, language, and denominational boundaries. It was sung at the Diamond Jubilee of Queen Victoria in 1897 and at a mass celebrated by Pope Paul VI in Yankee Stadium, New York, in 1965. It is so familiar in the English-speaking world that no one ever questioned singing this German hymn at the end of World War II to celebrate victory over Germany!

The tune, which has been matched with the text since it was written, appears in *The Hymnal 1982* in two harmonizations.

❧

"Thank you." It is a small phrase, easy to write or say. "Thank you" is an appropriate response when we receive a gift, not because it is proper etiquette, but because it is a natural thing to say. A gift, after all, is not just an object: it is an expression of love. We nurture love, our own and the giver's, when we express our gratitude. It is a dynamic that feeds the souls of both of us.

I must have been very young—probably less than three—when I made my first gift by carefully drawing a picture for my aunt on the back of a glossy red raisin box. A few days after my mother sent it off to her, I received a real letter, just like a grown-up, from the recipient, who said she was very impressed. (I imagine she was; it isn't every day that one receives a piece of a raisin box as a gift.) I remember as if it were yesterday the way I felt when I received that letter of gratitude. I had put myself into the gift, and it—and I—had been appreciated.

I continue to find joy in gift-giving. I shop for Christmas gifts all year long, stashing them away in a "present drawer."

I wrap them with excitement, thinking about how pleased the recipients will be to open this special thing I have chosen for them. When there is a wedding gift to buy, my husband and I never just rush out to check the bridal register; we discuss the couple and their life-style, and try to choose something unique.

But something has happened recently. Many of us seem to have lost the habit of saying "thank you." Givers are concerned that wedding presents might not have arrived, and wonder if the Christmas packages were stolen in the mail. It is sad, because an opportunity to connect with friends or relatives by giving—and responding—has been missed. It is sad that life can be so rushed that there is not time to enjoy the surprise of opening a gift, to feel gratitude, and to enjoy saying so.

I know that God does not need thanks. But our "thank you" to God feeds our souls. Like our "thank you" to friends who give us gifts, it should be the most natural thing in the world. And yet, for the same kinds of reasons, we often neglect our thanksgivings.

Martin Rinckart, ministering to his people in a plague-ridden, war-torn city, knew otherwise. He was able to write a hymn that expressed gratitude to God for life itself, and for the "countless gifts of love" God gave him. These gifts may have only been enough energy to conduct yet another funeral, or enough bread for another meal for his family— meager gifts in the world's eyes, like the picture on the raisin box. But in saying "thank you," Rinckart probably preserved his mental and spiritual sanity by fixing his attention on God's blessings rather than merely on the difficulties that surrounded him.

We can recapture the habit of saying "thank you" by

taking time to notice blessings, even in the midst of life's most difficult and rushed times. We can make sure that thanksgivings are included in our prayers, in church and at home. Taking time for gratitude for God's gifts is not a luxury. Our "thank you's" give us yet another gift: the gift of "ever-joyful" hearts, full of cheer and of blessed peace.

Index of Authors, Translators, and Sources

(Hymn numbers are in Roman type, page numbers in *italic*.)

Index of First Lines

Notes

1. Quoted in Mary Kay Stulken, *Hymnal Companion to the Lutheran Book of Worship* (Philadelphia: Fortress Press, 1981), 125.

2. Further ideas about alternative Advent and Christmas activities can be found in *To Celebrate: Reshaping Holidays and Rites of Passage*, published by Alternatives for Simpler Living, 3617 Old Lakeport Road, PO Box 2857, Sioux City, IA 51106.

3. S. Osborne, *If Such Holy Song* (Whitbey, Ontario: 1976), no. 153, quoted in Raymond F. Glover, ed., *The Hymnal 1982 Companion, Volume Three A* (New York: The Church Hymnal Corporation, 1994), 75.

4. *Our Hymnody: A Manual of the Methodist Hymnal* (New York: Abingdon, 1937), 484.

5. From a letter from Hugh Bancroft to Raymond Glover quoted in Glover, ed., *Hymnal Companion, Volume Three A*, 75.

6. The translations of the Latin "'O' Antiphons" are from A *Monastic Breviary* (West Park, NY: Holy Cross Publications, 1976), 218–219.

7. Quoted in Armin Haeussler, *The Story of Our Hymns: The Handbook to the Hymnal of the Evangelical and Reformed Church*

(St. Louis, MO: Eden Publishing House, 1951), 157.

8. Haeussler, 67.

9. *Songs of Praise Discussed* (London: Oxford University Press, 1933), 63.

10. Julian of Norwich, *Showings*, Chapter 86, translated by members of the Julian Shrine in *Enfolded by Love* (New York: Seabury Press, 1980), 59.

11. Albert Edward Bailey, *The Gospel in Hymns*, (New York: Charles Scribner's Sons, 1950), 144

12. Glover, ed., *Hymnal Companion, Volume Three A*, 117.

13. Haeussler, 181.

14. Glover, ed., *Hymnal Companion, Volume Two*, 637–38.

15. Haeussler, 523.

16. Daniel W. Patterson, *The Shaker Spiritual* (Princeton, NJ: Princeton University Press, 1979), 100.

17. *The Sonneck Society for American Music Bulletin*. Vol.XXIII, No.3, 72–73.

18. A. M. Allchin and Esther de Waal, *Daily Readings from Prayers and Praises in the Celtic Tradition* (Springfield, IL: Templegate Publishers, 1986), 14.

19. For a further resource, see David Adam's book, *The Eye of the Eagle: Meditations on the hymn "Be thou my vision"* (London: Triangle, 1990).

20. Esther De Waal, *God under my Roof: Celtic Songs and Blessings* (Oxford: SLG Press, 1984), 9.

21. Ibid., 13–15.

22. Albert C. Ronander and Ethel K. Porter, *Guide to the Pilgrim Hymnal* (Philadelphia: United Church Press, 1966), 248.

23. Gracia Grindal, *The Hymn*, Vol.39, No. 2, 28.

24. Evelyn Underhill, *Practical Mysticism* (New York: E.P.Dutton & Co., Inc., 1960), 3.

25. *Union Seminary Quarterly Review*, Vol.1, No.3, March 1946, 3.

26. Quoted in Joseph Robinson, "An Oboist's Bonhoeffer," *Union News: a Report to Alumni/ae and Friends of Union Theological Seminary in the City of New York*, Winter 1992, Issue No.21, 3.

27. Quoted in G. Leibholz, "Memoir", *The Cost of Discipleship* (London: SCM Press Ltd.), 1959, 13.

28. Samuel Willoughby Duffield, *English Hymns: Their Authors and History* (New York: Funk & Wagnalls Company, 1856), 272.

29. Thomas à Kempis, *The Imitation of Christ* (Mt. Vernon, NY: Peter Pauper Press), 10.

30. Ibid., 86.

31. Carlton R. Young, *Companion to the United Methodist Hymnal* (Nashville: Abingdon Press, 1993), 209.

32. Collect for Alcuin, *Lesser Feasts and Fasts* (New York: The Church Hymnal Corporation, 1980), 221.

33. Dietrich Bonhoeffer, *The Cost of Discipleship* (London: SCM Press Ltd. 1959), 35–37.

34. Erik Routley, *Christian Hymns Observed* (Oxford: A. R. Mowbray & Co.Ltd., 1983), 15.

35. Quoted in Winfred Douglas, *Church Music in History and Practice: Studies in the Praise of God* (New York, Charles Scribner's Sons, 1937), 210–11.

36. Ibid., 210.

37. Wesley Milgate, *Songs of the People of God* (London, 1982), 293.

38. P. Dearmer, ed. *Songs of Praise Discussed* (London,1933), 90–91.

39. Lionel Adey, *Hymns and the Christian "Myth"* (Vancouver: University of British Columbia Press, 1986), 167.

40. Glover, ed., *Hymnal Companion, Volume Three A*, 156.

41. Ibid., 156.

42. Catherine de Hueck Doherty, *Poustinia: Christian Spirituality of the East for Western Man* (Notre Dame, Indiana: Ave Maria Press,1975), 118–119.

43. Glover, ed., *Hymnal Companion: Volume Two*, 375.

44. Ronander and Porter, 32.

45. Tom Colvin, *Fill Us With Your Love* (Carol Stream, IL: Agape, 1983), 2.

46. Ibid.

47. Ibid., 4.

48. St. Teresa of Avila, *Interior Castle* (Garden City, NY: Image Books, 1961), 212–213.

49. Introduction to Bernard Katz, ed., *The Social Implications of Early Negro Music in the United States* (New York: Arno Press, 1969), xxi.

50. Clyde Owen Jackson, *The Songs of Our Years: A Study of Negro Folk Music* (New York: Exposition Press, 1968), 23.

51. *The Century Magazine*, (February 1895), quoted in Clyde Owen Jackson, ibid., 11.

52. Howard Thurman, *The Negro Spiritual Speaks of Life and Death* (New York: Harper & Row, 1947), 12.

53. Letter to Nancy Roth, December 31, 1992.

54. James Boswell, *The Life of Samuel Johnson* (New York and London: Oxford University Press, 1948), Vol. 1:265.

55. Stulken, 274.

56. Sean Caulfield, *In Praise of Chaos* (New York: Paulist Press, 1981), 13 and 15.

57. Ronander and Porter, 38.

58. T. S. Eliot, letter to Miss Nancy Moore, August 25, 1954.

59. Lewis Thomas, *The Lives of a Cell: Notes of a Biology Watcher* (New York: The Viking Press, 1974), 148.

60. Glover, ed., *Hymnal Companion, Volume Two*, 681.

61. Canon Ellerton, quoted in Ronander and Porter, 145.

62. Brain Swimme, *The Universe is a Green Dragon: a Cosmic Creation Story* (Santa Fe, NM: Bear & Company, 1985), 43–52.

63. Glover, ed., *Hymnal Companion, Volume Two*, 468.

64. Stulken, 273.

65. David Adam *The Edge of Glory: Prayers in the Celtic tradition* (Wilton, CT: 1988), 4.

66. John Julian, *A Dictionary of Hymnology, Vol. 1* (New York: Dover Publications, Inc., 1957), 386.

67. Ibid.

68. P. Dearmer, *Songs of Praise Discussed* (London, 1933), p. 331.

69. John Henry Newman, *The Dream of Gerontius and Other Poems* (London: Oxford University Press, 1914), 27, 30.

70. Erik Routley, *A Panorama of Christian Hymnody* (Collegeville, MN: The Liturgical Press, 1979), 205.

71. Adapted from Philip Schaff, ed., *The Teaching of the Twelve Apostles* (New York: Funk & Wagnalls, Publishers, 1885), 190–197.

72. Ronander and Porter, 335.

73. Quoted from the 1992 appeal sent by scientists to religious leaders: "Preserving and Cherishing the Earth: An Appeal for Joint Commitment in Science and Religion."

74. M. Scott Peck, *The Road Less Traveled* (New York: Simon and Schuster, 1978), 15.

75. John Wesley, *The Journal of John Wesley* (London: Robert Culley, 1909), 142–143.

76. Ibid., 475–476.

77. Kenneth W. Osbeck, *101 Hymn Stories* (Grand Rapids, MI: Kregel Publications, 1982), 130.

78. Frederick William Faber, *Hymns* (New York: E.P. Dutton & Company, 1875), 125–6.

79. John Julian, *A Dictionary of Hymnology, Volume II* (New York: Dover Publications, 1957), 1147.

80. Teilhard de Chardin, "Evolution of Chastity," *Toward the Future* (New York and London: Harcourt, Brace, Jovanovich, 1975), 86–7.

81. Julien Green, *God's Fool: the Life and Times of Francis of Assisi* (San Francisco: Harper & Row, 1985), 255.

82. Glover, ed., *Hymnal Companion, Volume Three A*, 15.

83. Pierre Teilhard de Chardin, *The Divine Milieu* (New York: Harper & Row, 1960), 89.

84. Gerard Manley Hopkins, *Poems* (New York and London: Oxford University Press, 1948), p.70.

85. Ibid.

86. Quoted in Ronander and Porter, 17.

87. Julian of Norwich, *Showings* (New York: Paulist Press, 1978), 279.

88. *Sister Wendy in Conversation with Bill Moyers: the Complete Conversation* (Boston: WGBH, 1997), 81–82.

89. Glover, ed., *Hymnal Companion, Volume Two*, 436.

90. From *Life and Letters of John Bacchus Dykes*, ed. J.T. Fowler (London, 1897), quoted in Glover, ed., *Hymnal Companion, Volume Three B*, 684

91. Margaret Drabble, ed., *The Oxford Companion to English Literature*, Fifth Edition (Oxford: The Oxford University Press,1985), 236.

92. Quoted in Ronander and Porter, 73.

93. Amy Lowell, "A Decade," in *Pictures of the floating World* (Boston: Houghton Mifflin Company, 1919), 94.

94. *Seven New Social Welfare Hymns*, The Hymn Society of America (New York, 1961), 2.

95. W. Osbeck, *101 More Hymn Stories* (Grand Rapids, MI: Kregel Publications, 1985), 90.

96. Ibid., 91.

97. Quoted in *A Sourcebook about Christian Death* (Chicago: Liturgy Training Publications, 1990), 3.

98. Glover, ed., *The Hymnal 1982 Companion, Volume Three B*, 665.

99. From "A Testament of Beauty", quoted in Edward Thompson, *Robert Bridges* (London: Oxford University Press, 1944), 106.
100. Adey, 142.

About the Author

The Rev. Nancy Roth has led numerous workshops and retreats in the United States and England on the subject of prayer. A native of New York, she taught music and dance before entering the General Theological Seminary in the late 1970s, where she was affiliated with the Center for Christian Spirituality. In 1981 she was ordained to the priesthood in the Diocese of New York. She was a consultant in Christian education at Trinity Church, Wall Street, where she taught courses on spirituality, and led a weekly meditation class at Manhattan Plaza, a residence for performing artists. From 1981 to 1983 she was program coordinator for Holy Cross Monastery in West Park, New York.

Her other books for Church Publishing include *Praying: a Book for Children* (1991) and *We Sing of God: a Hymnal for Children* co-edited with her husband, Robert N. Roth (1989). She is also the author of *The Breath of God: A New Christian Yoga* and *Organic Prayer* (Cowley Publications).

She and her husband, a retired church musician, live in Oberlin, Ohio. Nancy Roth continues to draw on her background in music, dance, and theology, both in leading workshops, classes and retreats, and in her writing projects.